E-COMMERCE 2017
Grow Your Business Selling on eBay, Amazon, Etsy, and Fiverr

Copyright © 2017 by Nick Vulich

Copyright © 2017 Nick Vulich
All rights reserved.
ISBN: 9781544198040

TABLE OF CONTENTS

ABOUT THIS BOOK 6
WHY LISTEN TO ME? 8
GET STARTED 10
SO WHERE DO YOU START? 11
ARE YOU GOING TO OFFER A PRODUCT OR A SERVICE? 12
BUILDING YOUR CLIENTELE 14
HOW DO YOU GET MORE ITEMS TO SELL? 15
YOU NEED TO KNOW YOUR NUMBERS 18

SELL IT ON EBAY 20
SO HOW DO YOU GET STARTED SELLING ON EBAY? 22
BE A BUYER FIRST, THEN BECOME A SELLER 23
WHAT SHOULD YOU SELL? 24
DIFFERENT WAYS TO SELL ON EBAY 26
FEES – HOW MUCH DOES IT COST TO SELL ON EBAY 28
HOW DO YOU SELL ON EBAY? 29
TITLE 29
DESCRIPTION 30
PICTURES 31
PRICE 32
EBAY TIPS AND TRICKS 33
BRAND YOUR EBAY STORE 33
AUTOMATE YOUR SHIPPING 34
ACCEPT RETURNS. 35
CREATE SPECIAL SALES 35
BE OPEN TO NEW IDEAS 35
DON'T BE AFRAID TO CHANGE DIRECTIONS 36
HOW TO LIST YOUR FIRST ITEM ON EBAY 36

SELL IT ON AMAZON 44
LISTING YOUR FIRST ITEM ON AMAZON 45
HOW TO ADD AN ITEM TO THE AMAZON CATALOG 47
AMAZON FBA 52
GETTING STARTED WITH FBA 54

FBA FEES 54
SELL IT ON FIVERR 55
THE VERY LEAST YOU NEED TO KNOW 56
GIG EXTRAS, THE KEY TO MOVING BEYOND $5.00 58
HOW DO YOU GET STARTED? 59
SELLER BASICS 60
CREATING YOUR FIRST GIG 62
FIVERR SELLING 101 68

SELL IT ON ETSY 71
GETTING STARTED 72
FEES 74
ETSY SHOP 75
SET UP HOW TO GET PAID 76
LISTING YOUR FIRST ITEM 77

KINDLE BOOK MARKETING 81
SO HOW DO YOU GET STARTED? 81
SUCCESSFUL BOOK IDEAS 82
YOU NEED TO PRODUCE A WELL-WRITTEN BOOK 83
GET YOUR MANUSCRIPT READY FOR PUBLICATION 84
PUBLISH YOUR BOOK 86
BOOK DESCRIPTION 87
TARGET YOUR BOOK 87
UPLOAD BOOK COVER AND BOOK FILE 89
PREVIEW YOUR BOOK 89
VERIFY RIGHTS AND SET PRICE 90
I'VE PUBLISHED MY BOOK, NOW WHAT? 91
HOW TO GET REVIEWS 92
KINDLE BOOK MARKETING 101 93
BOOK DESCRIPTION 93
KINDLE COUNTDOWN DEALS 94
AMAZON AUTHOR CENTRAL 95
FINAL THOUGHTS 96

BONUS EXCERPT 1 – SOCIAL MEDIA MARKETING MADE EASY 98
BONUS EXCERPT 2 – BOOKKEEPING MADE EASY 112

BONUS EXCERPT 3 – EBAY SHIPPING TOOLS MADE EASY 120
BONUS EXCERPT 4 – 25 TIPS & TRICKS TO BOOST YOUR SALES 129
BONUS EXCERPT 5 – USE KICKSTARTER TO FUND AND GROW YOUR BUSINESS 139
IF YOU ENJOYED THIS BOOK 150

ABOUT THIS BOOK

Several years ago, I started writing a series of books about how to maximize sales on eBay. Three of those books are *eBay 2014*, *eBay 2015,* and *eBay 2016*. Now I keep hearing from readers who wonder when I'm going to release *eBay 2017*.

After careful consideration, I've decided a name change is in order. eBay is no longer the single best choice available to online sellers. It is one of many marketplaces you can sell on. The choice comes down to what you sell, how you want to sell it, and how much freedom you want in presenting your product offerings.

Because of this, I've decided a more appropriate name for the new volume in this series is *Ecommerce 2017*.

No matter what marketplace you sell on, Amazon is the 800-pound gorilla. If you're not already selling on Amazon, you need to get started. ASAP!

I love eBay!

For sixteen years, I've been their biggest fan. I've taught tens of thousands of people how to sell on eBay. It always has been and continues to be, the best and easiest marketplace to sell on, but, and, this is the big but.

eBay has lost their direction.

eBay don't have a clear idea where it's headed. eBay is courting small sellers, but their marketplace and pricing are geared more towards larger sellers. Over the last several years, eBay has developed an anti-seller culture. With every move eBay makes, it becomes more difficult for sellers to make money using their platform.

Over the past year, the site has suffered numerous outages, errors in calculating shipping charges, and billing issues. Rather than resolve these issues, eBay raised its store fees this year by from 25 to 75 percent—depending on the level of store you have.

How crazy is that?

WHY LISTEN TO ME?

Hey there, Nick Vulich here.

If you're like me, I'm sure you're probably a little skeptical about taking advice from someone without knowing a little bit about them first.

I've been selling on eBay since 1999. Most of my online customers know me as history-bytes. I've also operated as *It's Old News*, Back Door Video, and Sports Card One.

I've sold 30,004 items for a total of $411,755.44 over the past fifteen years, and that's just on my history-bytes id. I've taken a break from selling on eBay and Amazon to concentrate on my writing and coaching, but I keep my hat in the game—constantly keeping in touch with sellers, and reading the latest reports on e-commerce.

I've been an eBay Power Seller, or Top Rated Seller, for most of the past fifteen years, which means I've paid my dues and met eBay's tough sales and customer satisfaction goals.

E-commerce 2017 is the thirteenth book I have written about how to on eBay. The first two, *Freaking Idiots Guide to Selling on eBay*, and *eBay Unleashed* are aimed more towards beginners. *eBay Subject Matter Expert* suggests a different approach to selling on eBay – building a platform where customers recognize you as an expert in your niche and buy from you because of your knowledge in that field. *Sell It Online* gives a brief overview of selling on eBay, Amazon, Etsy, and Fiver. *How to Make Money Selling Old Books & Magazines on eBay* talks specifically about what I know best, how to sell books and magazines on eBay. *eBay Bookkeeping Made Easy* helps sellers understand how to keep track of the money they are making, and how to take advantage of the tax code to make even more money. *eBay Shipping Simplified* helps sellers determine the best way to ship their items, and how to use eBay's shipping tools to make the task easier. It also has a primer on international shipping and using third party shipping providers such as Stamps.com and Endicia.

eBay 2015 (also known as *eBay Selling Advanced*) is my longest book to date and encapsulates everything sellers need to know to start and grow their eBay business. *eBay 2016* takes a different approach—showing sellers how to increase sales by employing a well thought out social media marketing campaigns using Facebook, Twitter, Pinterest, and other sites. It also takes a close look at blogging for online sellers, and how to fund special projects using Kickstarter.

This book is a serious rewrite of my book Sell It Online. Pretty much everything has been rewritten and revised with up-to-date information. It should help to help tie up all the loose ends so that you can sell successfully on any e-commerce platform.

Let's get started.

GET STARTED

Everyone dreams about making money online. Who wouldn't want a job where you can work at home in your jammies or underwear? A job where you don't have any bosses riding your rear end—telling you what to do, how to do it, or how soon to do it?

Selling online can be all of that and more.

Contrary to popular belief, it's not easy. No. You won't have the boss riding your tail, telling you what to do, but you will find yourself working harder than you ever did at your day job.

You will find yourself short on cash, especially when you are first starting out.

Just because you decide to hang your shingle out on eBay, Amazon, or any other online site, doesn't mean buyers will magically flock to your items, and shower you with cash.

Like anything else, successfully selling products or services online takes time—and money. Yeah! I started out with fifteen bucks and a dream, but more money would have opened up a whole new world of possibilities.

Anybody can go online, list a few items, and score a few quick sales. The key to being a successful online seller is duplicating this process, day in and day out, month after month.

This means you need to:

- Discover a stream of products you can sell over, and over again.
- Build a steady, and satisfied client base.
- Find a niche that sets your business apart.
- Stay one step ahead of your customers, and offer products they want, before they even know they want them.
- Understand your numbers. Too many online sellers believe raking in large sums of money means they are making a profit. Unfortunately, many of sellers discover too late; their profits the profits aren't what they expected because they forgot to factor in all their expenses.

SO WHERE DO YOU START?

One of the first things you need to do is decide what you want to sell.

Many first-time sellers try to sell everything but the kitchen sink. Most times, this strategy doesn't work well for them, because just like any other business, online businesses rely heavily upon repeat buyers. And, it's hard to attract repeat buyers, if you're selling old magazines one day, used tools another day, and toys another day.

If you want to build a successful online business that will grow and thrive over the long haul, you need to pick a profitable niche, and consistently offer products or services your buyers want, need, and are willing to pay for.

Let me repeat: **Pick a profitable niche**, and consistently offer products and services **your buyers want, need** and **are willing to pay for**.

ARE YOU GOING TO OFFER A PRODUCT OR A SERVICE?

What you choose to sell will determine which platforms you should sell on.

I'm going to look at three basic types of offers:

- Products
- Crafts
- Services

Products are tangible items. Some examples are books, clothes, electronics, collectibles, and toys.

Crafts are handmade either by you or by someone else. Examples are dolls, decorator light switches, floral arrangements, quilts, and custom made lingerie.

Services can be a combination of products and intangible items. Examples of services include product reviews, logo design, website design, tarot or psychic readings, custom videos, and similar items.

Products are better suited to selling on marketplaces such as eBay, Amazon, eBid, eCRATER, and bidStart. The reason for this is buyers come to these places to search for tangible products. Buyers are on eBay and Amazon shopping for things. They want new clothes, iPhones, iPads, shoes, toys, cars, etc.

Crafts can be sold on most online platforms. Your best bet is probably Etsy because it is a marketplace designed exclusively for crafts and vintage items. That's not to say craft items won't sell on eBay or Amazon. Etsy's creators designed the website to cater to Craft enthusiasts. The odds are it will draw the most sales for your stuff, but you need to test drive all three sites to determine which marketplace works the best for what you're selling.

Etsy's domination of the craft market could be at a turning point now that Amazon has opened its Handmade site. Only time will tell if the two services play well together, or decide to fight it out—mono-a-mono.

If you're unsure whether your stuff will sell better on one marketplace than another, run some tests listings to help you decide. The worst that can happen is your item won't sell. Maybe you're out ten or twenty bucks for your efforts, but you'll know what to expect. Guesses don't pay the bills. Sales do!

If you sell services, you need to be on Fiverr.

Fiverr is a marketplace where buyers offer their services for five bucks. Let me warn you; it's just crazy what some of these sellers are willing to do for $5.00. A small sample of the services offered on Fiverr includes logo design, blog writing, custom videos, product reviews, book reviews, and custom music videos.

And now, Fiverr is upping the stakes by allowing sellers to up their starting prices, build more extensive—and expensive bundles, and to charge a premium for commercial usage. It's a bold new world—making both buyers, and sellers wonder—What's next?

eBay is another solid choice for selling services. Compared to Fiverr, you should be able to command higher prices for your work, but the demand for services isn't as high as it is on Fiverr, so you're likely to get less work. Services I see thriving on eBay include logo design, web page design, eBay store design, and Facebook headers.

Carefully placed social media marketing, and pay per click (PPC) advertising are going to be essential to sellers if they want to make headway and drive sales in this market.

A good choice for service providers would probably be to offer your full services on eBay and to offer an abbreviated version of them on Fiverr to test the waters. We will go into this in much more detail later in this book.

BUILDING YOUR CLIENTELE

If you plan on being an online seller over the long haul, you need to build a steady stream of repeat buyers.

How do you develop repeat buyers?

The simple answer is:

- Offer unique products buyers can't find anywhere else.
- Give great customer service.
- Specialize (be an expert) in the products you sell.

With that said, how do you do these three things?

The fact is they all sort of blend together. When people recognize you as an expert in your product line, they feel good about spending their money with you. They will contact you with questions regarding authenticity, history, and value. At the same time, many of them will offer to sell you items, or be open to selling you the item they are inquiring about.

Customer service means promptly answering questions from your buyers, and not just with a "yes" or a "no," but answering their questions, and providing them with more information than they asked expected. Sellers need to add value every time they answer a question. A simple "yes" or "no" won't cut it. Not if you want to maximize sales.

Customer service means going out of your way to pack and ship your items professionally. Don't just toss them into a box or envelope. Carefully wrap everything you ship. Include instructions for care and handling of the items you sell. If your item requires installation, include detailed information about how to install it. Better yet, add links to an installation video, or embed it within your item description page.

Another way to position yourself as an expert in your field is to write books and articles on your subject matter.

Let's say you sell pre-1950 sports cards and memorabilia. You could position yourself as a subject matter expert by writing a series of short Kindle books on different card sets, or about how to grade cards, and when you should use a professional grading service.

Another idea here would be to make a print book using Create Space. For as little as $2.17 per copy, you can print a 100-page book that is professionally bound.

If you show your print book on every item description page and mention you are the author, that's even better. It will build instant credibility with your buyers. If you're selling high-dollar value items, you may want to include a "complimentary copy" with every qualifying sale.

This idea also works well for crafters and service providers. It will help you stand out from your competition.

HOW DO YOU GET MORE ITEMS TO SELL?

How you find inventory depends upon what you sell.

If you sell new items like electronics, books, or clothes, you can purchase most of your inventory from wholesalers. Most wholesalers require you to have a resale permit. Many of them also want to know a little more about the type of business you are in, and how you plan to sell the items you purchase. If you mention you sell on eBay or Amazon, some of them won't sell to you. You need to develop a game plan to approach wholesalers.

If you sell collectibles, you have a couple of options available to you.

Many hobbies have collectibles shows. Smart dealers grab a table, or two, at these events so they can purchase unique and one-of-a-kind collectibles. This works especially well if you advertise beforehand to let people know you will be there, armed with cash and ready to buy. Other dealers advertise in enthusiast magazines and local newspapers.

If you sell used clothing—yard sales and estate sales are a good way to pick up inventory on the cheap. The Salvation Army Store, Good Will, and other thrift stores normally have a great selection of new and gently used clothes you can resell at a good profit.

If you shop thrift stores, yard sales or estate sales for your eBay inventory check out this book. 9 Easy Ways to Start Making Money on eBay in 72 Hours or Less by Michelle Angell. She gives a great breakdown on how to approach each type of sale, and how to bargain for the best deals.

I've found lots of great items I can resell at Target, Wal-Mart, TJ Maxx, and Kohls. Many sellers work this strategy, and buy seasonal closeouts and hold them until the start of next year's season when they can sell them for higher prices.

If you decide to purchase most of your items during closeout sales at local retailers you should take a look at Barcode Booty by Steve Weber. Steve is an expert in online selling. His book talks about how online sellers can discover hot-selling products at local closeout sales by using barcode scanners and their cell phone or a PDA.

Scanning software makes it easy to snag profitable merchandise to resell. With the proper software, you can link your phone, or PDA, with the Amazon catalog. When you scan a barcode, it gives you the items product rank and selling price on Amazon. This way you can pick the products that sell right there, while you're in the store looking at them. People also use scanners at used book stores, and library book sales, to help select the few gems that will make them money.

If you want to try a barcode scanner application on the cheap, download the Price Check Android App on Amazon. There is also an iPhone app available.

Amazon designed Price Check as a comparison shopping tool for their customers to use when they are in stores, but you can use it to check values on Amazon to see if you can score a profit. The app lets you scan barcodes, type in the item name or UPC, speak the product name using voice recognition, or snap a picture and let Amazon's photo recognition software match it up. Within a few seconds, it tells you what the item is currently selling for on Amazon.

Give it a try the next time you're shopping the closeout aisles. See what you think!

Another sourcing idea that has worked well for me is scouring eBay listings for items I can resell. The reason this works is that so many sellers have no idea what they're selling, and many of them are just plain lazy (they don't describe what they're selling well, or they only include one picture, when five or six would sell the item).

Try it once. Pick a few categories. Spend fifteen or twenty minutes a day searching for items you think are underpriced or listed poorly. You should easily be able to locate five to ten items you can resell for a sweet profit.

Another idea I borrowed from Frankie on the *American Pickers* is bundling products to increase sales. The really neat thing here is bundling can work with just about any type of product.

Normally paperback books are slow sellers on eBay, but if you can pick up five or six books in a series by the same author and bundle them, many times, this will catch the eye of readers. Or how about if you grouped four or five books together on dieting and weight loss, or online selling, and list them at a premium price.

Second-hand clothes sellers can use the same tactic. Items you normally can't sell, do well when you bundle them into complete outfits.

Think of yourself as a value-added reseller, when you bundle items, and you will do well. Bundles can make your listings stand out if you price them competitively.

After you've been at it awhile, you will be able to develop a buying and merchandising strategy that works well for your online business.

YOU NEED TO KNOW YOUR NUMBERS

The absolute worst thing that can happen is for you go full blast into online selling thinking you're making beaucoups bucks because money keeps pouring into your PayPal account, only to discover later that it isn't so. Unfortunately, this happens way too often.

To make a profit in any business, you need to know your numbers.

There is a huge difference between money coming in, and making a profit. To make a profit, you need to make enough money to cover all your expenses, plus the cost of the items you are selling. Anything left over after covering all your expenses is your profit.

Sounds easy, doesn't it?

Here are just a few of the expenses you're going to have in any online venture:

- Cost of the goods you are selling
- Seller fees for using (eBay, Fiverr, Etsy, and Amazon)
- Internet provider fees
- PayPal or merchant account processing fees
- Packing supplies (boxes, envelopes, peanuts, bubble wrap)
- Postage (insurance, shipping, tracking fees)
- Collateral services (Auctiva, Vendio, Ink Frog – any similar tools you use to enhance listings or for picture storage)
- Advertising (Google or Amazon pay per click ads)
- Automobile expenses (gas, mileage – for going to post office, shopping for supplies, or purchasing inventory)
- Phone, fax, computer, scanner, digital camera
- Home office expenses (desk, chair, and expenses for remodeling your office.
- Home related bills (if you choose to claim the home office deduction, you can also deduct the portion of utilities, sewer, trash and other home-related expenses)

These expenses add up quickly, and if you don't keep careful track of them, you can easily fool yourself into thinking you're making a profit, when the truth of the matter is, you're losing your ass.

SELL IT ON EBAY

I can't believe it's been five years since I've started writing about how-to-sell on eBay. So many changes have taken place – on, and off, of eBay. And, there are more coming all the time.

Traditionally, eBay issues two seller-updates every year—one in the spring, and another in the fall. These updates are eBay's way of giving seller's a heads-up to let them know what's coming down the pipeline, and upcoming changes to the site.

eBay released the *2016 Fall Seller Update* not too long ago. Here is a quick run-down of changes sellers can expect.

- Active content is prohibited from the site beginning in June of 2016. That means no more videos or animations are allowed in auction listings. Overall, that's good. It brings an end to all those holiday templates with falling snow, flying reindeer, etc.

- eBay is tweaking performance standards - again. Buyer feedback, DSRs, and other incidents that are (resolved successfully with your buyer) will no longer count against you. eBay says they're going to concentrate on what matters most. What will count against you is seller canceled transactions, and cases that closed without seller resolution. Sellers who aren't meeting standards will have 90 days to get back in line.

- Return policies are changing. Beginning in October of 2016, sellers will have the option to exchange or replace items, rather than to just give refunds.

- Turbo Lister will take its final bow in June of 2017. Many of its features will become part of the new seller hub.

- Finally, category updates are ongoing. As eBay continues its move to be more like Amazon, sellers will need to update listings to add category specific information.

Overall, the changes reflect a more subdued eBay. The policies have moved away from "we're going to get you," to more of a "we're going to partner with you" style.

The *2016 Spring Seller Update* hit many sellers where it counts - in the pocketbook. eBay store prices took a hefty jump, in return for a larger allotment of free listings.

Basic store prices jumped to $24.95; Premium stores moved to $74.95, and Anchor stores jumped 0ver 75 percent to $349.95. For high volume sellers, the new price structure should come as a welcome change. For most sellers, it means a higher price to play.

- eBay is giving mobile a major boost They announced the end of active content in listings beginning in June of 2017 to provide mobile users a better experience. eBay also created a new view item feature for mobile. It culls a 250-character text-only description to show to mobile users. The idea is to provide relevant details—quickly, for time conscious mobile shoppers.

- In its move to be more like Amazon, eBay is expanding product reviews to more categories and products. Their research shows product reviews keep buyers on the site longer and increase sales as much as 18 percent.

Again, the updates come from a milder, but still money-grubbing website. While Amazon, and other online retailers, make their money on the backend, eBay continues to insist on taking their cut on both ends of the transaction.

That's not a problem—if they can draw more active buyers to the site, but until they do that, eBay needs to control its greedy ways.

SO HOW DO YOU GET STARTED SELLING ON EBAY?

Getting started selling on eBay is about as easy as it gets. The folks at eBay offer a lot of great tutorials, and the sell your item form walks you through a lot of the information you need along the way.

To begin selling, you're going to need to register for an eBay and PayPal account, if you don't already have them. To learn more about opening an eBay seller's account, click here. To get started with PayPal, click here.

eBay offers casual sellers fifty free auction listings every month. I would suggest you use them to list a few items. This way you can test the waters to make sure you're comfortable selling on eBay before you invest a lot of time, or money, into something you might not like.

Here's the bad news.

eBay places limits on new sellers. Getting started, you can only list ten items per month. Payments are held for twenty-one days, or until buyers leave positive feedback, so it's important to shine during your trial period.

The hold is automatically removed after 90 days, or when you make 25 individual sales or $250 in sales. If you're close to breaking out of your trial period, call eBay customer service - (866) 540-3229. Many times, they can make if possible for you to list more items sooner.

Selling on eBay can be a lot of fun, but it's not for the feint-of-heart, or someone looking to score a quick profit. Test the waters first, before you jump in with both guns blazing.

BE A BUYER FIRST, THEN BECOME A SELLER

If you've never bought anything on eBay, it's going to be hard for you to be a good seller.

The reason I say this is it's a lot easier to be a good seller once you understand why, and how, people buy stuff on eBay.

People shop on eBay for many different reasons. Some people shop on eBay because they're looking for items on the cheap. They want to wear designer clothes, but they can't afford to buy them new.

Collectors scour the eBay listings every day looking for that rare missing piece they want to add to their collection. These are the people sellers love to have bid on their auctions, because they get lost in their desire to have the item, and end up fueling a bidding frenzy.

Other people shop on eBay because they don't like going to stores. They're tired of pushy salespeople, crowded parking lots, and stores that run out of stock on the items they want. Shopping on eBay saves these people time and frustration.

Some people savor the excitement. For them buying on eBay is a lot like spending a day at the casino. They like to bid on items and win things at auction. It's the rush of excitement, and the thrill of winning these people are after.

You need to buy a few things first and experience some of these emotions before you start to sell on eBay. In the long run, it will help you to understand better what your buyers want, and why they are buying from you.

Another reason you need to be a buyer first is you need to rack up some good feedback before you start selling.

One of the great things about eBay is buyers and sellers can rate each transaction they participate in, and grade each other on a scale of from one to five. Sellers strive for five-star feedback because it offers social proof they are a reliable seller who delivers a great buying experience.

People are going to be leery of buying from you if you hang out your shingle and start trying to sell with a big old zero for your feedback rating. That zero is going to make potential buyers scream out. "Danger, Will Robinson! Danger!" because you are an unknown quantity. This is especially true if you're selling higher priced items or items where there are lots of sellers with awesome feedback offering similar items.

The easiest way around this is to buy a few things. Pay quickly, leave great feedback for your seller, and wait to receive feedback for your purchases.

My suggestion is to buy ten or fifteen small items over the course of a week. Once you have ten five-star feedbacks under your belt, it's time to get started selling.

WHAT SHOULD YOU SELL?

Deciding what to sell is one of the toughest decisions most new sellers face. It doesn't have to be.

Chances are you have great things all around you—things that have been collecting dust for a long time on the shelves in your attic, garage, or basement.

Walk around your house for a few minutes. Gather up five or ten items that are collecting dust in a closet or some other cubbyhole, and get ready to watch the magic begin.

Selling items you currently own is also a great way to de-clutter and get rid of all the stuff you've meant to throw away or sell at a yard sale over the years.

Do you have an old VCR that still works, but you never use anymore? Bundle it up with a stack of movies, and it could be a great seller. Many people still swear by VCR's—especially the older ones, because the newer ones no longer have built in tuners.

Be sure to tell people if your VCR has a tuner. You could get more money from it.

I have a junk drawer that has five or six old cell phones in it. Some of them work. Some of them don't. I bet I could bundle them up for a quick sale on eBay. What about your DVD collection? Have you stopped watching your DVD's because it's more convenient to watch movies on demand from your cable and satellite provider, or from Netflix? Bundle them up, and you can score some quick cash on eBay.

Old video games are another quick seller on eBay. If your kids are anything like mine, they've gone through five or six video game systems over the last several years, and now the old ones are stacked in the corners of their room or your living room. Sell those old game consoles on eBay and free-up some space.

Is your closet full of clothes you no longer wear? How about the kids? Younger kids outgrow their clothes every six months, or even sooner. There is a huge market on eBay for used clothing, especially name brands, or designer brands for adults or kids.

Are you beginning to understand? You probably have at least fifty to one hundred items sitting around the house that buyers on eBay would love to purchase.

Jump in and test the waters to see if selling on eBay is right for you.

DIFFERENT WAYS TO SELL ON EBAY

There are several ways you can sell your items on eBay. Over time you will want to add them all to your toolbox.

Auctions are what made eBay famous. Many items are listed starting as low as a penny. The final selling price is determined by what people are willing to pay. With a little luck and a great description, that penny starting price can turn into fifty, even one hundred dollars or more—if you can catch a wave of bidders.

Fixed Price listings are just like shopping at Wal-Mart or Target. Sellers list their item for sale. If a buyer wants the item, they can purchase it at the offered price.

Classified listings are a whole different animal altogether. They are used more by businesses than by everyday sellers. An example here would be if you are trying to sell a home or business. The idea behind a classified listing is to capture leads and get people to call or email you. With a normal listing, such as an auction or fixed price listing, sellers aren't allowed to include contact information—such as a personal email address, or a phone number. Classified listings provide a workaround for this.

Other types of businesses that use classified listings are website designers, and people selling specialty advertising, such as custom imprinted shirts and pens.

eBay has several add-ons that let sellers turbocharge their fixed price and auction listings.

Buy-it-now is an option sellers can add to items they are selling at auction. It lets buyers purchase an item immediately, rather than waiting for the auction to end.

eBay requires the buy-it-now price to be at least 30% more than the starting price. So, if you start your item at $10.00, your buy-it-now price needs to be at least $13.00. My suggestion is 30% is not a big enough jump.

When I run auctions with a buy-it-now, I shoot for the moon. If I start my item at $9.99, I set my buy-it-now price at $25.99. In one out of ten auctions that sell, I get the $25.99. If I'm selling a book I have a really good feeling about; sometimes I'll go crazy and set my buy-it-now price at $99.99, $179.99, or $249.99.

The cool thing is often my items sell for that outrageous number because I take the time to craft a great description that builds value for my book. I get that number even when other sellers are offering the same book with a $10.00, or $20.00 buy-it-now price.

Don't let yourself get suckered into playing the price game, and always offering the lowest price. It's all in how you position your items.

Best Offer is an option sellers can add to their fixed price listings. Best offer lets sellers be flexible on their asking price when they use fixed price listings.

Here's how it works. The buyer sets the price he wants for his item, then allows sellers to send him a best offer. Pricing can be a little tricky when you do this because the offers you get will be all over the board.

What I've found is you tend to get three types of offers:

- They lowball you at $5.00 or $10.00, no matter what your asking price is.
- They offer you half of your asking price.
- They ask for a few bucks off to cover the cost of shipping.

So how do you handle best offers?

I like to put my listings on auto-pilot whenever possible. That keeps eBay from sending me a bunch of low-ball offers. When you select best offer, eBay lets you set two options: 1) Is to decline all prices below a certain number, and 2) Is to accept all offers above a certain amount. By doing this, you only need to deal with the offers where you still have a chance to make money.

Sometimes, I'll just say what the hell! And accept the offer—even though it's a little less than I hoped expected. Most times I try to deal with the person making the offer to see if I can get them to bump their price up a notch or two.

The way I do this is to send them a counter offer, along with a short note. "Sorry, the best I can do is $15.00 plus shipping. It is a nice item in excellent condition." A counter offer throws the ball back into the buyer's court. They can decline my offer, or send back a counter offer.

You're going to end up closing the sale about fifty percent of the time when you send a counter offer, so you need to decide whether to take the first offer or to shoot for a better deal.

Another option is to set a **reserve price** when you are selling with the auction format. Unless you're selling a really valuable item, a reserve price is probably not the best option. A reserve price can make buyers think your item is over-priced. A better strategy is to set a starting price you can live with and take your chances. You've got to be fearless. If you get down to the last ten minutes and things aren't looking good, the natural response is to pull the plug and yank the listing, but that isn't always the best option. Often, the most heated bidding action takes place during the last five or ten minutes. Check how many people are watching your listing before you do anything.

FEES – HOW MUCH DOES IT COST TO SELL ON EBAY

Fees add up quickly when you sell on eBay. I've had many months where eBay's take from my earnings has been over $2,000.

There are two types of eBay sellers. Those with eBay stores, and those without eBay stores.

Store sellers pay a basic fee every month. In return, eBay provides them with a location to host their items and a set number of free listings.

There are additional fees for listing upgrades, such as buy-it-now, reserve auctions, and picture packs. For a complete breakdown of eBay fees, go to

http://pages.ebay.com/sellerinformation/news/springupdate2013/springfeesimplification.html

How do you sell on eBay?

Selling on eBay is easy once you understand a few of the basics.

To consistently make sales on eBay you need to master four tactics:

- Craft a great title.
- Write benefits driven descriptions of what you are selling.
- Include close-up pictures that showcase the item you're selling from every angle.
- Get the price right.

TITLE: Your title is the number one sales tool available to you on eBay. It's how people find what you're selling.

eBay gives you eighty characters to broadcast your message, so you need to get it right. The best strategy is to pack your title with keywords that help potential buyers find your item.

Don't worry about how your title reads.

It doesn't have to make any sense. What it needs to do is include all the possible combinations someone may use to search for your item. Your title should include the brand name, model number, version, year made, color, accessories included, new / used, warranty, and misspellings if there are any common ones.

Here are a few great titles for iPads currently listed on eBay:

- Apple iPad 3rd Generation 16 GB Wi-Fi + Unlocked (Verizon) 9.7" – Black

- Brand New Apple iPad 3rd Generation 64 GB White WI-Fi + 4G (AT & T) 9.7" White (MD371LL/A)
- Apple iPad 3rd Generation 16 GB Wi-Fi Cracked Screen, Works
- Apple iPad 3rd Generation 16 GB Wi-Fi MC705LL/A Fully Functional Cracked Screen

DESCRIPTION. Good descriptions tell buyers everything they need to know about the item.

Your description should tell potential buyers who made the item, what the model number is, the color, the size, and what condition it's in. Is it new? Is it new it the box with tags? Is it gently used, but in like-new condition?

Put yourself in the buyer's shoes for a moment. What would you need to know if you wanted to buy your item? If you're unsure about what details to include, look at what other sellers say about similar items they have for sale. Make a few notes, and include some of the better information in your description.

Be upfront about condition related issues. Is there a scratch? Is there a chip in the paint? Are there some light grass stains on the knees of those jeans?

Be your worst critic? Point out all the flaws in the items you're selling. Better people should learn about any problems with your item before they buy it than after it arrives on their doorstep. The last thing you want is negative feedback, or to have to pay return shipping because you didn't properly describe your item.

Here are a few great descriptions, to give you an idea of what you should say:

"1954 was the first year when Hank, featured in the Topps #128 Hank Aaron baseball card, played as an outfielder for the Milwaukee Braves. A smart photograph of Hank Aaron with his full name and autograph is featured on the front of this 1954 card. The back of this Hank Aaron baseball card supplies you with all his vital information and other major league records. Due to his immense popularity, this Hank Aaron baseball card is nearing the top of the record books in baseball history. Fun and amazing, the Topps #128 also makes a perfect gift for the baseball fan."

"You are bidding on an original 1958 Topps Mickey Mantle card #150. Look at the quality of this card, NICE! It is 100% authentic, and unaltered—guaranteed! This card has absolutely no creases, the corners have a nice form with tip touches, the centering is superb, has perfect clear imagery, has deep rich colors, has shiny original gloss, is clean, and the card has awesome eye appeal. There are no pinholes, markings, paper loss, stains, or any other damage of that kind. It's a beautiful card of one of the game's greatest players. It's a keeper. The card shown is the one you will receive. Please check out the images. The quality of the card will speak for itself."

They're great descriptions. They tell a good story. What sets them apart, even more, is many of the sellers in the sports card category post only one or two pictures, with no description.

These guys make more sales because they take the time to craft killer descriptions.

PICTURES. Pictures sell items. Make no mistake about it, very few people are going to buy your stuff if you don't include at least one picture. More pictures are always better.

Ask yourself this. Would you shell out $400 for a used laptop if you couldn't see a picture of it first? Probably not.

Suppose I'm selling a rare Hummel figurine, and my description says it's in mint condition except for a small chip at the bottom of one leg. What would you think if I only showed you one picture of the entire figurine? You'd probably have some lingering doubts about that chip, wouldn't you? As a seller, I could have easily closed the deal by including several close-up pictures of the chipped area. Several well shot, close-up pictures would make it easy to determine whether the chip is a bid stopper or not.

You need to take a good look at every item you sell. Put yourself in the buyer's shoes. What parts of the item would you need to see to decide if you want to buy that item? For a baseball card, you obviously need to see the front and back of the card. If you're buying a laptop, you'd probably want to see a picture of it with the Windows logo displayed on the screen as proof that it works. You'd also want to see a picture showing any accessories included with the laptop—cords, case, manuals, discs, and anything other goodies.

If you sell clothes, check out how some of the most successful sellers do it. They model their clothes on male and female manikins. It gives potential buyers a better frame of reference for what they're buying than just looking at a flat picture of a blouse or pair of jeans. They include close-up pictures of designs and any flaws they described.

PRICE. Price is important when you're selling on eBay, but it's just one piece of the puzzle. If you've taken the time to write an amazing title, craft a description that sells, and include plenty of close-up pictures, you're entitled to ask for a premium price.

Too many sellers let themselves get caught up playing the price game. They get stuck with the mentality people only shop for price.

Most buyers are willing to pay a little more if you give them a compelling reason why they should spend it.

Think about the last time you shopped one of the big-box stores for a big screen TV. You probably went to the store because the ad featured a 42" TV for $349.00. The salesman likely asked you a few questions before he showed you that one. On the way to it, he stopped at a 50" Smart TV so he could show you how easily it hooks up to the internet through your Wi-Fi connection. He might have mentioned how easy that makes it to watch movies on Netflix and Hulu. Did he hand your kids a pair of 3D glasses so they could get a good look at the dinosaur popping out of the picture?

What happened next?

Odds are you bought the $999 Smart TV, or the more expensive 3D TV because it had all those great features you hadn't considered.

eBay buyers aren't any different than shoppers at a big-box store. They might have every intention of grabbing the least expensive book or pair of jeans when they start shopping, but if you can give them a compelling reason to spend a little more, they're willing to open up their wallets and let a little more cash spill out.

My point is: If you're happy getting the same price everyone else is getting, go ahead and use the same lame-ass description everyone else is using. If you want the big bucks, think of each of your listings as a work of art. Craft a compelling description that will make people beg you to take their money.

EBAY TIPS AND TRICKS

Now, I'm going to share a few secrets with you to help you step your game up a bit, so you can save time, and make more money selling on eBay.

BRAND YOUR EBAY STORE. One of the best things about eBay is sellers can brand themselves on the site. You can display your business name and logo in each of your listings. You can create a custom listing template and storefront that projects the image you want your customers to see.

eBay stores level the playing field and make it easier for you to compete with the big guys. They let you look like a big business, even if you're a one-man operation working part-time from your kitchen table.

A custom storefront gives you the opportunity to offer your customers a unique shopping experience.

eBay sellers can create custom pages to share information and product details with their customers. The problem is very few sellers use them.

That's a big mistake!

Custom pages can greatly improve your customer's shopping experience and your sales. Here are a few ideas based on how I've seen eBay sellers use their custom pages:

- Include a sizing chart for clothing that explains how customers should take measurements.
- Show the measurements associated with each size for men's, women's, and children's clothing.
- Explain how your items are packaged and shipped (this is especially important if you have an upcharge for shipping because of the extra care you take in packaging items).
- Tips on how to take care of the items you are selling.
- If you sell custom items, like imprinted clothing, pens, or mugs, explain what information you need from customers to make the project happen.
- Tell your story. What drove you to get into this business? What makes your business special? Why should customers buy from you rather than one of your competitors?
- If you sell graded sports memorabilia, explain what grading is, and the different grading services you use.
- If you sell collectibles, you can explain how you grade your products.
- Design custom landing pages for different groups of your products.

AUTOMATE YOUR SHIPPING. eBay and PayPal have some useful shipping tools integrated into them, but once you start selling more items, or if you are selling on multiple platforms, you're going to want a more advanced tool.

Stamps.com is run by the United States Post Office and can help sellers mail their products more efficiently. Stamps.com users can easily import buyer information from eBay, Amazon, Etsy, and other marketplaces, then print shipping labels on their home computers.

The reason I use Stamps.com is they let me ship first class international packages without having to go to the post office. If you use the tools available in eBay, PayPal, and Amazon, the only international shipping options available to you are Priority International and Express International (both of which are far too pricey for the items I sell).

ACCEPT RETURNS. If you want to play with the big boys, you need to act like them. No one likes returns, but everyone likes to make more sales. Accepting returns is the best way to encourage more people to buy from you.

When I first started ramping up my sales on eBay, I offered "a 100% Money Back Guarantee. No questions asked."

Over the last fourteen years, I've had less than ten returns. Probably fifty people have requested to return something, but after I let them know it wasn't a problem, and I'd be happy to take their item back, most of them decided they would rather keep the item.

Try offering a return policy, and see how it affects your business. If it doesn't work out for you, you can always change your policies down the road.

CREATE SPECIAL SALES. Use *Mark Down Manager* to create special sales for your customers, or to sell slow moving inventory. *Mark Down Manager* is a tool available to eBay store owners. You can access it in the *Marketing Tools* section of *Selling Manager*.

Sellers can use *Mark Down Manager* to discount items by category selectively, or they can go through and select individual items to put on sale. How many items you can list for sale depends on the level of eBay store you have.

It's not a sure thing. Sometimes it works better than others, but it's worth a shot if you need to raise some extra cash fast.

BE OPEN TO NEW IDEAS. Customer wants and needs change over time. Your eBay business needs to be flexible so you can change with them.

Keep tabs on your competition, and watch what they are doing.

Hang out where your customers do online and offline. Listen to what they are saying. Are their favorite websites featuring new products? Pay attention to the trends you see happening, and try catering to them. You don't have to jump on the bandwagon and go at it full blast but take a few baby steps, now and again. Try selling some new items. Some of them will work out. Some of them won't. The important thing is over time you will be carrying more products your customers want, need, and are willing to buy.

DON'T BE AFRAID TO CHANGE DIRECTIONS. If you've given it your best shot, and it's not working, don't be afraid to change directions. Maybe you need to change the way you're branding yourself or presenting your product. Maybe you need to kiss the old product line goodbye and reinvent yourself with a whole new product line.

There's no shame in reinventing your business. Most people will reinvent their career at least three times over the course of their work life. Why should your eBay business be any different?

HOW TO LIST YOUR FIRST ITEM ON EBAY

Now it's time for a quick walk through about how to sell on eBay.

The easiest way to start a listing is to search for the item you want to sell. Underneath the gallery pictures at the top of the listing page, you will see -

$ Have one to sell? Sell it yourself

Click where it says, "Sell it yourself," to bring up the sell your item form. It will walk you through the process, and you will have your item listed in no time.

Category determines where your item is slotted on eBay. Make sure it's the correct category for what you are selling. Research suggests 80% of buyers search by the item name, but the other 20% browse categories to discover new items when they are shopping. If you list your stuff in the wrong category, you're going to miss the opportunity to sell to these people.

Title. You get eighty characters to describe your item. Be sure you make it keyword rich, and loaded with terms buyers will use to search for your item.

Subtitle is an optional feature and costs from .50 to $1.50 depending on the style of listing you are using. If you're listing a unique or a high dollar value item, using a subtitle may be a good choice. Keep in mind people can't search by the terms you include in your subtitle. Its main purpose is to give buyers a little extra information so they can decide whether to click on your listing or not.

Subtitle does cost extra so only use it when you think it can help sell your item. Another thing to keep in mind when you use a subtitle, or any other listing enhancements, is when you relist your item, you're going to pay that extra fee again and again.

Be sure to keep track when you use listing enhancements, and remove them before you relist your item if you no longer want to use them.

Condition description lets you make a quick comment about any condition related issues with your item. What I like about it is it shows up right at the top of your listing. When you add comments here, tell people all the faults your item has, but be sure to word it, so you minimize your item's faults.

If you're selling a rare book, you could word it like this, "This book has a few small pencil marks scattered throughout the first three chapters, but none of them interfere with reading the text. Other than this, the book is in very nice condition." Notice what I did. I told potential buyers the book had some defects (pencil marks), but otherwise, it was "very nice." When you word your description this way, it creates the perception the problem you listed isn't that bad.

Item Specifics change based on the item you are selling. In most categories, you're not required to fill these out but if you do it can help you come up higher in search when people filter their search by size, color, etc.

Pictures. eBay gives you up to twelve free pictures with each listing. All pictures are required to be:

- At least 500 pixels on the longest edge. eBay recommends 1600 pixels for the best picture quality.
- Borders are not allowed around pictures.
- Sellers cannot add any text or artwork to their photos
- At least one picture must be uploaded for every listing, even if you sell using eBay's catalog.

Gallery Plus is a listing enhancement available for pictures. It costs 35 cents per listing. I wouldn't recommend it unless you have something special that will benefit from an expanded gallery picture.

Description. Enter your item description in plain text or HTML.
If you use a template, you should paste it into this box, and make whatever changes you need to customize it for each listing.

Themes. Themes are a form of template. eBay charges ten cents for each listing with a theme. My advice is to pass on themes. If you want to use a template to spruce up your listings, sign up for a service like Auctiva or Ink Frog. They host your pictures and include a wide selection of free templates.

Choose how you'd like to sell your item. Do you want to sell your item at auction or fixed price?
Both methods have their place. When it first started, eBay's main focus was on auctions. Over the last five years, most of the action

has shifted to fixed price listings, where there is no bidding. People just click on the item and purchase it.

Everyone has their preference about which listing format is better. Much of it comes down to what you're selling.

If you're listing a unique item or something where the selling price is not well known, or frequently fluctuates such as hot concert tickets or collectibles, the auction format should bring you a better price.

For commodity items or items that normally sell in a close price range, fixed priced listings are a better choice.

If you have an item that is selling well, you may want to vary the length of your listings. Try one day, three days, five days, seven days, and thirty-day listings. Include buy-it-now on all your auction listings, and use a higher price for your fixed price listings. This strategy will maximize your sales and the final selling prices you receive for them.

If you're selling in the auction format, enter your starting price. If you want to include a buy-it-now price, list it in the appropriate box. Below that enter how many items you are selling. In the radio box for the duration, select how long you want the listing to run.

Schedule start time allows you to decide what time your item should start selling. eBay charges an extra ten cents to use this feature. My thought is there are plenty of buyers out there for your item whenever you decide to start and end it. Some people swear between 5:00 and 8:00 pm is the best time to end your listings, other people insist Sunday is the best day. It's your dime - pick a strategy you like and run with it.

eBay Giving Works lets you sell your item for a charity. When you sell with Giving Works, you can donate anywhere from 10% to 100% of the selling price to your favorite charity. When your item sells, eBay will credit you back a portion of the selling fees.

The nice thing about selling with eBay Giving Works is they have thousands of local charities signed up. Chances are you can easily discover ten or twenty local charities to support in your neck of the woods.

Charity listings draw more page views. In my experience, I often receive two to three times as many page views when I sell for a cause.

Getting Paid. PayPal is eBay's preferred payment method. It's linked to eBay, and most people are comfortable using PayPal. Another thing to remember is your customer doesn't have to have a PayPal account to pay with PayPal. They can enter their bank or credit card info into the secure form and make their payment without ever signing up for PayPal.

Shipping details. There are two sections you need to work with here. One is for domestic shipping (in the country you are in), and the other is international shipping (to foreign countries).

You have four shipping methods to choose from:

- **Flat rate shipping** means you charge the same shipping rate to everyone regardless of where they live. If you have a small item, such as a postcard or a book, you can tell everyone you will ship it for a certain amount. Sometimes it will cost you a little more, sometimes a little less. The good thing is flat rate shipping is easy to understand. If you say $4.00, everyone pays $4.00 for that item to be shipped.
- **Calculated shipping** means you input the weight of your item into the shipping details; then eBay automatically calculates the shipping cost to each buyer's location. The shipping fees your buyer pays depend upon how much it costs to ship the item to them. When eBay displays the shipping amount, they figure it based upon what it would be for that particular buyer. Calculated shipping beneficial if you live closer to a buyer because your shipping could be less expensive than that offered by sellers who live further away.

- **Freight** is calculated for shipments over 150 pounds. Freight shipping is for larger and heavier items that need to ship by an over-the-road truck line.
- **Local pickup** means the buyer can pick the purchase up at the seller's location. Sellers select this option when the stuff they're selling is very fragile or is bulky and hard to pack. I've seen buyers use it with furniture, exercise equipment, or when they are selling a large collection of books. Because the items are large and difficult to pack sellers often, don't want to go to the trouble and expense of doing it, so they limit shipping to local pickup only.

International shipping. Many sellers are afraid to offer international shipping because they're not sure how it works. International shipping isn't any more difficult than shipping in your home country. The major difference is you need to include a custom's label with most international shipments, that lists the contents of the package, and its value.

Your local post office can walk you through it the first few times, or if you are printing shipping labels online, the program will walk you through all the steps.

One thing I would suggest with international shipments is to set delivery expectations for your customers. When you mail a package, send a quick email to your customer to tell them their shipment is on the way. You may want to say something like this in the email, "Thank you for your order. I mailed it today. Normal international delivery time is two to three weeks, but can take as many as six to eight weeks depending on customs and local post offices." Doing this will save you a lot of customer service emails with customers who don't receive their packages the next week.

eBay also has something called the Global Shipping Program. It makes shipping items internationally as easy as mailing within your home country. To opt into the program, you select the Global Shipping Program under the international shipping options when you're listing your item. When an item sells internationally, eBay notifies you to send it to one of their shipping partners within the United States. When the package reaches the shipping center, your responsibility for it is over. The shipping center repackages the item, fills out customs forms, and sends it on its way.

Other things you'd like buyers to know. The first item here allows you to set bidder requirements, such as not allowing bidders with two or more recent non-paying bidder strikes to bid on your auctions.

If you have a sales tax permit, select the state you want to collect sales tax in and the amount to collect. If your item sells in that state, eBay will collect tax on the item for you, and list it separately on the invoice for you and your buyer.

Return policy. eBay doesn't require you to accept returns, but I would strongly recommend doing so. It will increase your sales. If you decide to accept returns you need to check the boxes, and state how soon the buyer needs to return the item, and who pays return shipping – the buyer, or the seller. You should also state a return policy in the box provided. Mine is, *"Here at history-bytes we understand buying items sight unseen on the internet can be scary at times, for this reason, we offer a 100 % MONEY BACK GUARANTEE. You can return your item within 14 days for a full refund – No Questions Asked."*

The final box on this page gives you a chance to list any additional checkout instructions. Normally all I say here is "PayPal is the only payment method we accept."

At the very bottom of the page, it will show you **your fees so far**. After this, click continue to move on to the next page.

At the top of the next page, eBay takes one more shot at selling you some of their listing enhancements such as gallery plus, subtitle, and bold. My advice is just to say no! Unless you have something special selecting any of these options is going to be just like throwing your money down the garbage disposal.

At the bottom of this page, it will once again review your fees. If everything looks good, click on list your item, and it will go live on eBay. If you want to see how it looks first, click on preview listing, and it will generate a preview of your listing for you to review.

....

Selling on eBay can be easy, fun, and profitable.

My advice is to baby-step it. List a few items you have around the house. If you decide eBay is a good fit for you, start looking for a niche you can fill, and target products to it.

Build your business slowly. Keep testing new products, discard the losers, and keep the winners. Over time you will build a strong business with a steady stream of repeat buyers looking for the new products you have added.

SELL IT ON AMAZON

Amazon is the proverbial 800-pound gorilla when it comes to e-commerce. Every online marketplace is trying their damnedest to emulate their success.

Unlike eBay and many other online commerce sites, Amazon doesn't have separate listing fees for the items you put up for sale there. Sellers can add thousands of items to their Amazon store without putting up a penny until they sell something.

Another great thing about selling on Amazon is you can list most of your items in one minute or less. There's no need to snap any pictures or write a detailed item description. Selling your item on Amazon is as simple as hitching a ride on the Amazon listing page.

It's easy to spot the items listed by individual sellers. When you see a box like the one below, the items being sold by Amazon are listed under the Amazon price. The items offered by individual sellers are in the next two categories—used and new.

What I want to do first is take a minute to walk you through listing a typical item for sale on Amazon. Then I will come back and give you some pointers about how you can maximize your sales there.

LISTING YOUR FIRST ITEM ON AMAZON

Type the name or the description of the item you want to sell into the Amazon search bar. Click on the item you want to sell. Off to the right-hand side, you will see a small box labeled **more buying choices**. At the bottom of this box click on the **Sell on Amazon** button.

At this point, you're eight steps away from listing your item for sale on Amazon.

Step 1. Amazon shows you the title and picture of the item you selected and asks you to verify this is the correct item you want to sell. If it's the correct item, you don't need to do anything.

Step 2. Tell people what condition your item is in. Click on the radio button in the box labeled **condition,** and select the one that best describes the condition of your item.

Below this, you have a chance to add a comment about the condition of your item. If you are selling a textbook, you could say "overall very good condition, but it does have some highlighting in the first three chapters."

Step 3. Amazon shows you the lowest price listed for your item. Next, it shows the lowest shipping price available for it. What you're going to find in most cases, especially if you are selling new items is Amazon has the lowest price, and shipping is free (with

Amazon prime). Don't panic! People will still buy from you, even if you have a higher price, and charge shipping.

Step 4. Enter your selling price. Next, to the box where you enter your selling price, Amazon will show how much they are going to charge your customer for shipping.

Step 5. Tell Amazon how many of this item you have available for sale.

Step 6. This step tells Amazon to collect taxes if you have enabled them to do so. For most casual sellers, you're going to skip this step, so don't worry about it.

Step 7. Enter your SKU (short for stock keeping unit). It's how you identify the item you are listing for sale. During my peak selling period, I had over 10,000 items listed for sale on Amazon. All of them were numbered and stored on storage shelves. Whenever one of them sold, I could go to that shelf, and easily pull the item for shipping.

When you're just starting out a SKU doesn't seem all that important, but if you intend to grow your business, you need to start thinking about some labeling system as early in the game as possible. It will keep you from having to backtrack or rework your listings down the road.

If you decide not to enter a SKU, Amazon will assign one for you.

Step 8. Select your shipping methods. Amazon requires you to add a basic shipping service. I would suggest choosing Expedited Shipping (priority mail), and the first international shipping option (first class).

Press the yellow **Continue** button at the bottom.

Review your selling information. The last few boxes show you Amazon's commission when your item sells, how much Amazon allows you for shipping, and how much money you will receive (including your shipping credit) after Amazon's commission is taken out.

If everything looks good, press the **Submit your listing** button.

The next thing you're going to see is Congratulations! You've successfully listed _____.

That's it. Your item is live on Amazon.

Sit back and wait for the sales to start rolling in, or better yet, list more items so you can make more sales.

That's all there is to selling on Amazon.

HOW TO ADD AN ITEM TO THE AMAZON CATALOG

If you sell unique items that aren't already in the Amazon catalog, Amazon lets you add item description pages to their catalog. While it's not hard to do, it does take a little extra time and effort, so I'm going to cover this in more detail.

To add an item to the Amazon catalog you need to visit Seller Central and hover your mouse over **Inventory**. At the drop down menu select **Add a Product**.

Search the Amazon catalog to see if it is already listed. If your item is not currently available on Amazon, you can add a new item by clicking **Create a new product**.

Select a category. To do this, you can either search for a category or browse through a list of categories. Choose the category that most closely fits your item.

After you select the category, you want to list your item in you will be taken to the sell your item dashboard.

The trick here is to provide as much information as you can under each of the six tabs you see at the top of your dashboard. Try to fill in every box you can, because Amazon will use the information you give to show your item in relevant search requests.

At the very least, you need to fill in the boxes with a red star to the left of them.

Vital Info. What you put here is going to become the title for your listing. Make sure it is keyword rich and describes your item properly. You have 250 characters to get it right and let potential buyers know what you're selling. Make the most of it. Give the name, manufacturer, model number, color, accessories, and other important information.

Manufacturer is what it says. If you know who made your item, list it here. If you know the brand name, enter it in the next line. Enter the model number and manufacturer number if they are available. Package quantity means how many of them are packaged together – one, two, or a dozen. The UPC or EAN are the manufacturer's product code. If you know the UPC code, enter it here.

Offer. List your selling price. Below that, you can create a sale price. If you enter a sale price, select when you would like the sale to run. Enter how many items you have. If you have a sales tax permit, enter the pertinent tax info, so Amazon can collect sales tax from your buyers.

Handling time refers to how many days it will be before you ship the item. Amazon's default is one or two days. If you need a longer lead time, specify it here. An example would be if you are working with a drop shipper, and it takes some time for the order to process through their system.

Selling date is the day you want Amazon to start showing your item. Gift options. Will you gift wrap the item, or include a card with it? Select the services you wish to offer. Restock date means if you are out of stock, when will more be available.

Import designations specifies country of origin. Several choices are available. Read through, and choose the one most appropriate for what you are selling.

Next, you need to choose your shipping method. You can choose to ship the item yourself or to offer Fulfillment by Amazon (FBA). FBA means you shipped your products to Amazon when you listed them, and Amazon is handling shipping and fulfillment for you. The biggest advantage here is your items often qualify for Amazon's free shipping offers including those with Amazon Prime. Another advantage is many buyers are more comfortable buying from you because your item ships to them directly from Amazon.

I will talk about Fulfillment by Amazon, and how it can help to increase your sales, in more detail later in this chapter.

Images. You need to include at least one photo of your item. The more pictures you include, the easier it is to sell your item. Picture requirements are listed next to the uploading tool.

When you get your pictures ready to upload, you should keep in mind:

- Only show the exact item you are selling. Don't include any extra items or props in your pictures.
- Watermarks are not allowed.
- You cannot superimpose any text over your images.
- Your main image must be a photo. Drawings are not allowed.
- All pictures should be a minimum of 1000 x 500 pixels. Buyers cannot zoom in on smaller images, so they will not have close-up views of what you are selling.
- J-Peg illustrations are the preferred file type.

Description. The description section is broken down into two sections. One is for product features, and the next section is for your actual written description of the item.

Features provide bullets, loaded with bite-size information about your item. Here are some of the features given for the Apple iPad to give you an idea what type of features you should list with your items:

- Apple's newest generation of iPads

- 9.7 inch (diagonal) LED Glossy back-lit screen
- Forward facing and rear cameras
- Apple IOS 10 and access to Apple Apps store
- 1 GHz dual-core Apple A5 custom-designed processor

Your description should be feature and benefit rich. Write it in a narrative style. Everything should be product focused. Amazon doesn't allow you to include any information about your business.

After you list your item, the item description page becomes part of the Amazon catalog. Any seller with the same item can list it alongside yours on the same item description page.

Keywords. Keywords are tags you can add to your items to help buyers find them in search.

Search terms are where you enter the keywords buyers use to search for your item. Include all the obvious ones: Product name, model #, manufacturer, color, and size. If you're not sure which keywords to use, check the Google Keyword Tool. It will help you pick keywords people use to search for your item.

Try not to use single word search terms. Use "long tail keywords" whenever possible. Long tail keywords are more specific in nature and encompass most of the searches made on Google. Some examples of long tail keywords are: "Space exploration in the Milky Way Galaxy," "How to write better keywords," and "How to make money on Kindle."

More Details. This section lets you add more product specific information about your item. Some of the categories include: Brand, MSRP, Part number, model number, is your item subject to prop. 65 reporting in California, shipping weight, product and shipping size specifications, and the like. Specific information asked for is based on the type of product you are selling.

Press **save and finish**. In no time at all, you're item will be live on Amazon.

It sounds complicated, but after you've added two or three products to the catalog, it will be a whole lot easier.

The biggest problem I have when I add custom pages is there's no real-time preview like you have on eBay. It can take a half hour or more for the listing page to display on Amazon, so you need to check back later to make sure everything posted okay. Another problem when you're adding pictures is it can take ten or fifteen minutes for them to upload, so you're stuck waiting before you can work on your next product listing.

That pretty much covers listing your items on Amazon.

If you have a large catalog of items, you can upload them through a spreadsheet. There are also services that help eBay sellers move their entire eBay store to Amazon.

One service I've had experience with is Export Your Store.

What I like about using Export Your Store is they do all the heavy lifting for you as far as moving your items from eBay to Amazon. The bad thing about using Export Your Store is Amazon is nothing like eBay. After they transfer your items to Amazon, you need to optimize everything for selling on Amazon.

Here are a few of the differences between eBay and Amazon that can cause you problems.

- Amazon is a marketplace. They don't allow personal branding or HTML code in any of their item description pages.
- Amazon doesn't allow references to your business in their item description pages.
- Amazon requires tags (keywords) to be entered in the proper section of their listing form to help buyers find your item in search.

The folks at Export Your Store are really good at stripping the HTML code out of your listings, and getting them moved over to eBay. I had over ten thousand items exported from eBay to Amazon in just over two days.

Then I started receiving a stream of item violation warnings from Amazon. When I imported my eBay items, you could still have your customer service email address in your listings. This violated Amazon's terms of service, so I was forced to go through just over 10,000 items, one at a time, and edit each of them individually.

What followed was three weeks of pure hell, spending twelve to fourteen hours of every day, checking, revising, and deleting listings.

A few other things I discovered while editing my listings was sometimes when they stripped out the HTML code from my listing templates; they also removed part of my item descriptions including the SKU numbers I used to locate items once they sold. I had to add keywords to every single Amazon listing (I think this was because I sell one of a kind collectibles, and each item required adding a new page to the Amazon catalog). If you're selling more traditional items, like electronics, books, CD's, or DVD's that already have a catalog page, this would not be an issue.

Despite all the problems I mentioned, I would still recommend Export Your Store. Customer service was responsive, and they worked quickly to resolve my problems. The current charges for exporting your eBay store to Amazon start at $99 for the first 1,000 items and work up to $249 for up to 15,000 items. These are per month fees that keep your inventory and prices synched between the two sites.

Several other companies can help you export your eBay store items to Amazon. Two of them are Vendio and Linnworks.

AMAZON FBA

Amazon FBA (Fulfillment by Amazon) can help skyrocket your sales. Sixty-four percent of people who have used Fulfillment by Amazon have increased their sales by 20% or more.

When you use Fulfillment by Amazon, Amazon becomes customer service central for your business.

Here are the top benefits you receive by using FBA:

- Your items become eligible for FREE Super Saver Shipping and Amazon Prime Benefits,
- Your FBA items are displayed with no shipping charges, giving you the benefit of being a lower priced seller.
- Your back end is taken care of by Amazon. They handle all the shipping, returns, and customer service problems for you.
- Your items become eligible to compete for the Buy Box.

By using FBA, you free up more of your time to source new products, and to enjoy life more.

You ship your inventory to Amazon's warehouse. Once they check your items in and receive them into their inventory, they go live on Amazon. Each time one of your items sells, you will see it show up in your seller dashboard, but the good folks at Amazon do all the heavy-lifting for you. They collect your payment. They ship the order for you, and they handle all customer service issues or returns.

Compare that with being an eBay Top Rated Seller who is required to ship their item with a one-day handling time to receive their 20% final discount fee. The eBay seller is chained to his computer, while the Amazon FBA seller is free to enjoy his life without the constant rush to ship and handle customer service issues.

FBA is also a great deal for Amazon buyers.

FBA assures customers a great experience when buying from you. Most of the items sold through FBA are eligible for Amazon Super Saver Shipping, and other Amazon Prime Benefits, including free shipping on orders over $49.00 ($25.00 for qualified books).

GETTING STARTED WITH FBA

To get started using FBA:

- List your items in seller central, and select Fulfillment by Amazon as your shipping choice.
- If you already have the item for sale on Amazon, go to **Manage Your Inventory** on your Seller Central Dashboard. Select the product that you want to include as FBA.
- Print the labels provided by Amazon to ship your items to their warehouse.
- After Amazon receives and scans your items into their inventory, they go live and are ready for sale.

FBA FEES

For more detailed information on FBA fees, you can visit the Fulfillment by Amazon Guide. (These prices are current as of 12/01/2016. Be sure to check with Amazon for the most current prices.)

The very least you need to know is:

- There is a pick and pack fee of $1.00 per item.
- There is a fee by weight starting at .47 per pound. Amazon charges a storage fee based on the cubic feet taken up by your items.
- The fee is 54¢ per cubic foot from January to October, and $2.25 from November to December.

SELL IT ON FIVERR

Fiverr is a freelance marketplace where buyers and sellers can exchange cash for services. What's amazes me is every item featured on Fiverr is $5.00—almost.

There appears to be no limit to the types of services sellers can offer on Fiverr. Among the recent gigs (what Fiverr calls listings) are –

- Custom logo design
- Facebook header design
- Amazon book reviews and product reviews
- Puppet videos
- Kindle and eBook book covers
- Tarot readings
- Psychic readings
- Resume and cover letter writing
- Poetry Writing
- Business card design
- Infographic design

By now hopefully, you get the idea. If you can imagine it, you can find a way to offer it as a gig on Fiverr.

THE VERY LEAST YOU NEED TO KNOW

Fiverr is relatively new to the e-commerce scene.

Micha Kaufman and Shai Wininger founded the company in 2010. Every gig starts at $5.00, but that's changing as the site continues to reinvent itself. Sellers receive $4.00 for each completed gig. Fiverr's take is twenty percent or $1.00 from each five-dollar gig.

As of October 2016, there were over three million gigs listed on Fiverr.

Fiverr has a leveling system, like eBay's Top-Rated Seller Program.

- **Newbies** have limited options on Fiverr. They can offer two gig extras limited to $5.00, $10.00, and $20.00. New sellers are limited to accepting four gigs in one transaction.

- **Level One** status opens up more opportunities for sellers. To reach Level One status, sellers need to complete ten gigs in the previous thirty days with a minimum 90% satisfaction rating. After they level up, sellers can list up to 15 gigs at a time, offer "fast delivery" for extra profits, and provide custom orders up to $1500. Level One status also opens up another gig extra—for a total of three and allows sellers to accept eight orders in one transaction.

- **Level Two Sellers** are required to have completed 50 gigs in the last sixty days with a minimum 90% satisfaction rating. When they reach this level, sellers have the chance to increase their income significantly. Buyers can purchase up to twelve of their gigs at one time. Gig Extras jump to five, and the price range jumps to $5.00, $10.00, $20.00, and $40,00.

- Becoming a **Top-Rated Seller** is like receiving tenure at a major university. The process for reaching this status is somewhat mysterious. The Fiverr blog states the site editors "mutually" choose top Rated Sellers. What is clear though is once you receive this designation a whole new world of profit possibilities open up to you. Top-rated sellers can charge up to $100 for each gig extra, and they receive the Top-Rated Seller Badge next to each of their gigs.

If you're serious about making money on Fiverr, you need to level up as quickly as possible. The easiest way to do this is to offer a large selection of gigs and provide excellent customer service.

GIG EXTRAS, THE KEY TO MOVING BEYOND $5.00

Earlier I mentioned gig extras.

Gig extras are the method Fiverr has devised to let sellers take their income to the next level. To better understand how gig extras work, check out these extras offered by Professor Puppet.

Get more with my Gig Extras

☐ I will post your video on YouTube so you don't have to OR Deliver your video in 1080p HD PLEASE SPECIFY Requires no additional time	+$10
☐ I will superimpose your URL or any message over your video Limit 2 supers per upgrade Requires no additional time	+$10
☐ I will Shoot your video on my Green Screen and superimpose a different background Requires no additional time	+$50
☐ I will RUSH SERVICE. I will drop everything and make your video FIRST before anything else in the queue Requires no additional time	+$20

Even though every gig starts at $5.00, Professor Puppet can increase his take to $95.00 if someone adds all his gig extras to their order.

And, just in case you think most buyers stick with the basic $5.00 offer, think again! Professor Puppet has made two promotional videos for my businesses. Each time, I spent over $35.00.

So, if anyone out there is still wondering how you can make money selling each of your services for only five bucks, you know the answer – **GIG EXTRAS**. They can easily raise your average $5.00 sale to $25.00, or more.

One final thought on gig extras. The best gig extras don't necessarily have to cost you more time or money.

Most sellers offer very simple gig extras:

- Next day service for five, or ten dollars

- A PSD file of the graphic they already designed for an extra $5.00 to $20.00. It's no extra work – you already have it on your computer.
- Two extra revisions for $5.00, or $10.00.
- Your video delivered in additional formats for $10.00, or $20.00.
- A 3D cover to go with the 2D eBook cover they already designed for an additional $5.00.

The key to making the most money on Fiverr is to keep your gig extras simple and easy to perform, but still, make them appear valuable to your customers.

I saved the best part for last. Many sellers dangle a new-fangled cyber tip jar out there that lets them collect even more money.

Do you want to make even more money? The key is to give customers a compelling, or downright crazy reason to give you an extra-large tip.

One seller suggests an extra $5.00 would let him start his day with a latte from Starbucks, for $20.00 he could put a half a tank of gas in his old jalopy, and for $50.00 he would have a good start at taking his wife out for a romantic supper.

Who could resist giving this creative genius a tip?

HOW DO YOU GET STARTED?

Getting started as a seller on Fiverr is as easy as entering your email address and choosing a username and password. That's it, and you're a member of the Fiverr community.

Before you click the join button, take a few moments to think about your username. It is how people will come to know you on Fiverr.

A relevant username that complements the service you are providing will help to position you as an expert in the service you are offering.

Many people choose the first idea that pops into their head, or maybe their name. The thing is, if you name your business marysue or wonderwoman 113, people aren't going to have any idea what you do.

If you call yourself videoreviewer or bestlogodesigner, people are going to know right away what services you offer. A professional username can help position you as the right seller.

SELLER BASICS

Every gig on Fiverr starts with the words "I will ____ for $5.00."

As a seller, your job is to fill in the blank. Just what is it you're willing to do for five bucks?

I know, some of you are saying – not much.

A recent Fiverr survey says there are thousands of sellers making $1000 to $2000, or more, every month selling their services on Fiverr. Some of the elite sellers make $5000 or more each, and every month.

So, before you turn your nose up at five bucks, let's examine some of the things you need to consider before creating your first gig.

Before you do anything, check the Fiverr website for two or three days. Explore the different categories, and click into as many gigs as you can.

Keep your pen and notebook handy. Whenever you see something you like or something, you think you might want to do – jot it down.

Write down the seller's username – the title of their gig – keywords they use to describe their gig – any special instructions they include in their descriptions. It's important information you can use to craft your gigs.

Don't stop there. Check out the pictures, or samples they include. If the seller has a video describing the service they are offering, watch it, and make a few notes about what they say, and how they describe their gig.

Study the feedback left for gigs similar to yours. What did buyers like, or dislike, about them? Look for clues to help you design a better gig, and position yours, so more people will choose to do business with you.

You don't have to pick out your first gig right now, just get down as many ideas as you can.

Look over the gigs you examined.

Draw a star by the ones you think would be a good fit for you. Cross off the ones you don't think would be a good fit for you, or you can't see yourself doing.

This is where the rubber meets the road. At this point, you should have at least five gigs you think would give you a great start on Fiverr.

Make sure the gigs you choose are something you can make money doing.

Most sellers agree to make money you need to offer a service you can complete in no more than fifteen minutes. Five minutes or less is even better.

At fifteen minutes per gig, and an average profit of $4.00 per gig, that means you can make $16.00 per hour. If you can lower your working time to ten minutes per gig, you can make $24.00 per hour.

Now go back and evaluate the gig ideas you picked out. Be brutally honest.

Is this something you can do in fifteen minutes, or less? If not, is there a way you can do it faster? If not, scratch this gig off your list, or move it to your work on later pile.

Continue to evaluate each potential gig the same way.

If you're sure, you can complete them in fifteen minutes or less, great! Add them to your list of must do gigs.

The last step is to work a couple of your potential gigs to make sure how fast you can do them. Use a stopwatch to track your time.

Make a list of your gigs by how much time they took you to complete.

Pick the gig you want to get started on today.

From here on out we're going to concentrate on getting this gig ready to post on Fiverr.

CREATING YOUR FIRST GIG

Posting a gig on Fiverr consists of nine simple steps.

For this demonstration, we're going to assume you're going to sell a Kindle book cover. As we walk through the steps, take some time to reflect on each step, and how the process relates to creating your gig.

The gig shown below was created by one of my favorite cover designers. Right now, she has 86 covers waiting in her queue over the next three days, so you know this lady is breaking her ass to get them done, but at the same time, she's making some serious bucks.

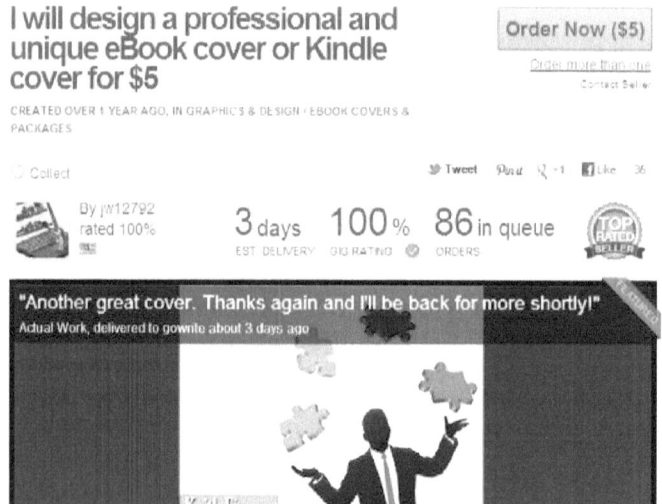

To get started, choose the Start Selling button at the top of Fiverr's main page.

Step 1. The first thing you're going to see are the familiar words, "I will _____ for $5.00."

Tell people what you're willing to do for $5.00. A good gig title should be short, tell people exactly what you are going to do for them, and be rich in keywords.

Look at the title for this gig. "I will design a professional and unique eBook cover or Kindle cover for $5.00."

It's a great title. It contains three main keywords "design," "eBook cover," and "Kindle cover." It also has two descriptors or adjectives "professional" and "unique."

The right keywords will give it a great shot at being picked up and shown by Fiverr's search engine every time someone searches for either "eBook cover" or "Kindle cover."

Step 2. Select a category. The beautiful thing here is Fiverr makes selecting a category super-easy. They only give you twelve choices: Fun & Bizarre, Online Marketing, Graphics and Design, Advertising, Writing & Translation, Lifestyle, Business, Programming & Tech, Other, Music & Audio, Gifts, and Video and Animation.

Choose the category that will give you the best bang for your buck.

Step 3. Description. Tell your story. Tell people what you are selling, what the benefits are for them, and what information you need from them to make it happen. If there are things you cannot, or will not do, this is the place to say it. A lot of sellers that offer art and writing services specify they won't write or draw pornography. Remember, it's your business, and what you choose to do, or not do, is up to you.

Let's look at the description in our sample listing.

"Over 5,000 covers created to date! 3D Covers are FREE, and when I say three days, I mean three days – regardless of the orders in the queue…and I'm not happy until you are so UNLIMITED

REVISIONS! Order now! * I also create covers for ALL genres, so let's hear what you have in mind. What makes my covers stand out from other designers here on Fiverr? I treat your cover as an individual! Are cars the theme of your book? How do metallic fonts and backgrounds sound? Chocolate the theme? We'll make book buyers want to lick the cover itself! Trust me; you'll love your cover. Order now!"

What do you think?

This description offers so many examples of the things you should try to include in each, and every one of your gig descriptions. The seller tells you twice, to "Order Now!" She tells you once in the middle of the description, and again at the end.

She emphasizes her covers are different from those made by other designers on Fiverr. Then she tells you what makes them better and different – "We'll make book buyers want to lick the cover itself!"

She guarantees buyers will be pleased with their cover. "I'm not happy until you are so UNLIMITED REVISIONS!"

Take some time to read through the descriptions written by many different Top Rated Sellers, and you'll quickly learn the secrets to being more successful and selling more gigs on Fiverr.

Step 4. Instructions to Buyer. Tell buyers what information you need to put their gig together.

Fiverr uses this box to request information from buyers, so before you fill it out, take a few minutes to carefully decide what information you need to make the buyer's project come together. The clearer you are with your instructions, the easier it will be to complete your project in as little time as possible.

Another benefit will be better feedback because you completed your gig on time, and how the buyer wanted it.

Step 5. Tags. Tags are simply a list of keywords people use to search for your gig on Fiverr.

ebook cover books design web kindle dsn

An easy way to pick your tags is to see what keywords other sellers are using to tag their gigs. Choose the keywords you think are relevant, and add them here.

Step 6. Maximum days to complete. What's the longest it will take you to deliver the finished gig? As a new seller, you should strive to deliver every gig within twenty-four hours.

People like fast. Everybody wants to buy something today and get it yesterday. Many buyers will choose your gig over someone else's when you offer one day service, especially when other sellers list a three to five-day turnaround.

Only offer one-day turnaround if you can deliver on it. You will hurt your rankings and increase your chances of receiving negative feedback if you deliver late. If you're not sure you can deliver your gig in one day, decide how many days you think it will take you to complete your gig and then shoot to deliver as soon as you can. That will give buyers a pleasant surprise, and happy buyers mean good reviews.

Step 7. Add image. Upload images to illustrate your gig. These should be the best samples of your work. For illustrations, Fiverr recommends a .jpeg format, 600 pixels wide x 370 pixels high, with a maximum file size of 5 megabytes. Once you have your pictures ready, you can use MS Paint or another graphics program to resize them to 600 x 370 pixels.

It is also recommended you upload a video. It can be something as simple as you talking about how you produce your gigs, giving instructions on the information you need from the seller to bring their gig to life, or a collage showing your gigs and comments from the people who purchased them.

Keep it simple. Be informative. Better yet, make it humorous.

Step 8. This item requires shipping. If you are sending a physical product to buyers such as a small craft, check this box.

Step 9. Press the **Save** button.

Before you decide press save, take a few minutes to look it over first.

- Did you spell everything correctly?
- Did you include enough keywords in your title and description?
- Are your tags or keywords ones that buyers will use to search for your gig?
- Did you include all the information you're going to require in your information request line?

When you're happy with everything, press **Save** and your gig will go live.

Pretty simple, right?

Here are a few things you should keep in mind as you begin your career on Fiverr:

- Sellers can list a maximum of twenty gigs at one time. Choose the gigs you offer carefully. Make sure they are gigs you can complete the quickest, and that will sell the best.

- When you are first starting out, you're only allowed to offer two gig extras, but many sellers have found a clever way around this. They suggest buyers should purchase an additional gig if they want something extra. For example, if your gig is to write a 200-word SEO article for $5.00, you could mention that buyers "should purchase an extra gig for every additional 200 words." It gives you the same benefit as being able to offer a gig extra.

- Be careful about the types of gigs you offer. Reviews and testimonials are big business on Fiverr, but offering to write a bogus book or product reviews for Amazon items is against Amazon's terms of service. What you will discover is many of these reviewers have a very short lifespan on Fiverr, because they quickly get shut down.

- Always offer a great value for the money you are charging. It will come back to you in good reviews and more business over the long haul.

- Spend at least a half-hour every week checking through the gigs offered on Fiverr. Look for new trends and services you may not currently be offering. It will help you to grow your business, and keep your offerings fresh and relevant.

FIVERR SELLING 101

Fiverr continues to reinvent itself, as the freelance marketplace evolves. Gigs are no longer required to start at $5.00, but most buyers offer a $5.00 gig as a gateway to more expensive offerings.

We've already talked about gig extras. Depending upon your seller level they give you an amazing opportunity to boost your income while customizing your gigs to meet buyer wants and needs.

Package attributes is a relatively new feature that can boost your sales.

If you've spent any time on Fiverr, you probably know what I'm talking about—even if you don't recognize the name.

	$5 Basic	$10 Standard	$15 Premium
Description	Basic Package	Premium Package	Pro Package
	A front cover of the book	A front cover, back cover and spine of the book	A front cover, back cover, spine and 3D image of the book
Back & Side	–	✓	✓
3D Image	–	–	✓
Delivery Time	2 days 1 day (+$5)	3 days 1 day (+$5)	3 days 1 day (+$10)
	Select $5	Select $10	Select $15

What I like about package attributes is they make it easy for buyers to compare your offerings. You can offer a basic product for $5.00, a step-up for $25.00, and a bigger step-up for $50.00. Most sellers are going to pick the middle option. They don't want to go to cheap, but they don't want to blow their whole wad either.

Package attributes make it easier to convert lookers into buyers because you're offering them more choices. I don't have any specific proof, but my guess is package attributes convert better than gig extras.

Experiment with your listings, and discover what works best for you.

Custom Offers are where the real money is at on Fiverr. Forbes Magazine did a story about four sellers who make $15,000 a month, or more, by using custom offers. One of the ladies profiled in the article runs an executive resume writing service. She went from making $5.00 per gig to making over $300,000 last year. A lot of her business comes from creating custom resume packages and selling them for $500 to $800 each—all by sending custom offers.

Think you can't do it? Think again.

Suppose you're a graphic designer who sells custom book covers on Fiverr. Create your listing just as you normally would. Add package attributes and gig extras to up-sell regular buyers. The only thing I want you to do differently is to add an additional line at the top and bottom of your item description page. It can be as simple as, "Are you looking for an eye-shattering design? Contact me for a *Custom Offer*."

That throws it back into the buyer's court. Some of them are going to be curious, and contact you. When they do, ask a few well-placed discovery questions, and fire off an offer to let them know what you can do for them.

Fiverr Anywhere works hand in hand with *Custom Offers* to help you make larger dollar sales.

Fiverr Anywhere started out as a Google Chrome extension. Since then it was moved to the Fiverr site. To access *Fiverr Anywhere* go to the Promote Your Business section under the My Sales Tab. Click on the Generate *Custom Offer* tab, then create your custom offer. After you've done that, you can retrieve your link. That will let you add your offer to your website, blog, email, or social media sites.

When someone contacts you, it works just like a regular *Custom Offer*. Potential buyers can accept your offer, or request a modification.

Use *Fiver Anywhere* and *Custom Offer* to grow your business and reach new buyers off the Fiverr website.

Good-luck! And, great selling on Fiverr!

SELL IT ON ETSY

Etsy is a community of crafters who get together to buy and sell handmade items. Sellers can also offer crafting supplies and certain vintage items.

A visit to the Etsy home page reveals several subtle differences compared to eBay and Amazon. Etsy has all the normal product pictures towards the top of the home page.

Below that are three featured Etsy *shops worth exploring.* Today's featured shops are RVS handcrafted, Fabric Shoppe, and Gretade Parry Design. A quick click on any of the pictures takes you to the Etsy shop. Gretade Parry Design is a perfect example of personal branding. The banner features three pictures of Gretade working on her products. Below that, you'll see another picture of Gretade in her work apron, followed by her product listings. Very nice.

As you scroll further down the page, you'll find a link to several featured sellers, along with a blog post featuring the seller, their family, and some of the products they sell.

Today's featured seller is Kathleen Smith, and her husband Justin, better known on Etsy as Smiling Tree Toys. After you click on the link, you're taken to a photo interview loaded with pictures of Kathleen, Jeff, and their children, who are pictured making some of their custom wooden toys.

Just below this is a clickable banner; that asks "What is Etsy." Want to know more? Just click on the link, and it'll explain everything.

The site has a folksy down-home feeling, and it pervades the everything you see on Etsy. It's friendly, inviting, and both, buyer and seller oriented – Something eBay used to be back in the day before they started kissing up to the big sellers.

Etsy's focus is on helping artists, crafters, woodworkers, and other makers of handmade items sell their wares. Sellers are also able to offer crafting supplies, and vintage items if they are over twenty years old.

GETTING STARTED

To get started look for the big red button that says Etsy in the upper left-hand corner. Click the gray button next to it that says **register** and fill in the required information.

As with all e-commerce sites, the most important decision to make when you register is your username.

I encourage you to take some time on this. Your name should tell people a little bit about your business, and the type of products you sell. Many people on Etsy choose to use their name, and that's fine, too. On Etsy, your brand is all about you, and the products you make.

After you're signed up, you should begin to fill in your profile so buyers can get to know you better. In the upper right corner, you're going to see a link that says **Hi username**. Click on that. It will bring you to Etsy's profile page. Click where it says **edit profile**.

The first thing you should do is add a profile picture. I suggest a photo of you, surrounded by some of your crafts, or of you working on a project. If you're feeling a little shy and don't want to include yourself in the picture, pick one of your favorite projects and upload a picture of it.

Continue filling out this form. Add as much information as you can. If you want to change your username, you can change it here. The last few lines at the bottom of this section let you select where you would like to share your profile information. By default, Etsy puts a check by these, so your profile information will show up in as many places as possible. Uncheck any information you would rather not share.

Over to the right hand, side of the screen you will see your control panel. Click on settings, and continue adding information to your profile.

- **Account**. If you have a Facebook or Twitter account, you can link them to your Etsy account here. You can also update your email address, password, or close your account.
- **Preferences** allow you to set contact information and other such info from Etsy. Use this area to set your location and currency preference. At the top, you can choose to filter out mature (XXX) items so that they won't show up in your search results. Etsy has them filtered out by default, so you need to turn them on if you wish to receive mature selections.
- **Privacy** allows you to select who can see your favorites, and if people can search for you by your email address or not.
- **Security** gives you additional methods to help secure your account online. All of them are switched off by default, and you must manually turn them on.
- **Shipping address** is just what it says. Enter your full mailing address here.
- **Credit cards** lets you put a credit card on file with Etsy.
- **Emails** allow you to select your email settings, and what emails you would like to receive from Etsy, and from your customers.

The next section is **Apps**. As business picks up remember to buzz back here now and then, and download apps to help you grow your business.

Here are a few apps I've had the chance to try out. They will give you an idea of what's out there:

- Fanpageology: When Etsy Meets Facebook
- Etsy8: An app for Windows 8
- Pict is an app that allows you to snap a picture, share it with your social network, and sell.
- EtsyFu an app that allows you to schedule Twitter posts to promote your business
- Direct Mail Manager for Etsy

Make sure you bookmark this page. It's loaded with useful tools you can integrate into your Etsy business.

If you have a website, there's a really cool tool named **Etsy Mini** that lets you build a widget so you can sell your Etsy items on your website.

FEES

Etsy fees are inexpensive and easy to understand. There is a listing fee of .20 for each item, and they run for four months. When your item sells, you pay a 3.5% final value fee.

At the end of the month, you receive a bill for your fees. All payments are due by the 15th of the month.

What's really nice is the good folks at Etsy haven't raised their selling fees in at least the last three years that I've been selling there. Take that, eBay and Amazon.

ETSY SHOP

All sellers can open an Etsy Shop. Your shop is your personal spot on the Etsy where you can brand yourself and your business. Etsy has a guide to help you get started. Click here to see the shop manual. http://www.etsy.com/help/article/246?ref=help_home

You should also visit the seller handbook. Click here to see it. http://www.etsy.com/blog/en/category/seller-handbook/

The manual does a good job of walking you through setting up and customizing your Etsy Shop.

Follow these steps to set up your shop:

- **Give your shop a name**. Remember what we said earlier. Make it unique, and make sure it describes your business. Barring that, use your name.
- **Upload a banner** to customize your shop further. Picture requirements are 760 x 100 pixels. If you're unsure where you can get a banner made, Fiverr has some great designers. They have a lot of designers that will make you a fantastic banner starting at $5.00.
- **Add a shop announcement**. The first 160 characters of your shop announcement are what show up in search when people search for your item using Google, Yahoo, and Bing. Make it short, descriptive, and compelling, so it will entice searchers to click on your shop.
- **Add shop sections**. This section is similar to categories in an eBay store. You can add ten sections to call out different product lines, items, or sizes.
- **Add shop policies**. Share information with your customers about how you do business. The main thing to remember is to keep your messages customer friendly. Too many sellers use strings of negatives words like "I don't," "I won't, "Checks and money orders will not be accepted."

It's ok to say what you will, and won't do, but find a nice way of saying it. People don't like it when you tell them what they can and can't do. They like to hear "this is what we can do for you."

Specific policies you can include are Welcome Message, Payment Policy, Shipping Policy, Refund Policy, Additional Information, and Seller Information.

SET UP HOW TO GET PAID

To set up your payment methods click on the **Get Paid** tab.

The first option you see is Direct Checkout. This option lets buyers pay for items through Etsy using their credit or debit cards. Etsy charges 25 cents per order, plus 3% of the order total for using this service.

If you're a new seller, Etsy makes your funds available to you within three days, or as soon as you ship the item, whichever comes first. Once you've been selling for 90 days, you can withdraw funds the next business day.

You can add additional payment methods by checking the link under the direct checkout box.

Additional payment methods include PayPal, Money Order, Personal Check, and Other. Make it easy on yourself, just accept PayPal. That's how 99% of your buyers will pay. If you decide to accept checks or Money Orders, allow 7 to 10 days for them to clear the bank before you ship your customer's purchase.

LISTING YOUR FIRST ITEM

Now that your shop is set up, it's time to list your first item.

- **Who made it?** Choices are: I did, a member of my shop, or another company or person. Select the one that applies.
- **Categories**. Use the drop-down menu, and select the category that best describes your item.
- **Add variations**. Variations are differences in your product listings such as size, color, etc. When a buyer selects your item, they will be required to choose the variations they want.

Keep in mind; variations don't show up in search. If you want the size, color, etc. to be searchable, you should set up a separate listing.

- **Photos**. You can add up to five photos to your listing. Make sure they are good clear photos that show all the details of what you are selling. If you have fancy frill work or designs, include a few close-ups of it.

Invest in a light box so you can take well-lit, close-up photos. You can find them for $30 to $40 on eBay and Amazon. What a light box does is help to diffuse the light so you can take a good clear picture of your item. Most light boxes come with several backdrops in a variety of colors to bring out the contrast in your pictures.

- **Title**. The key to writing a good title is to understand your title is the search string for your listing. It is how people find your listing on Etsy.

Think about every feature your item has. What terms will buyers use to search for your item? How else will they search for it? What period is it from the renaissance, 70's, 90's punk? Pick out the most important terms you can think of and pack them into the title.

- **Description**. Tell people what your item is. How it was made? What makes your item special compared to everybody else's?

Give people a compelling reason to buy your item. Tell them what's in it for them. If it is hand stitched, tell people. Let people know how you made it, or what materials you used to make it.

The more detailed information you include, the better chance, you will have of selling it.

- **Shop section**. If you set up shop sections, which section do you want to include it in.
- **Recipient**. Identify likely buyers. Most times you will want to leave this one blank. The reason is you don't want to limit your chances to sell it by targeting just one type of buyer.
- **Occasion**. Will it be used for a special event? Like recipient, leave this one blank, unless you are sure it is for only one occasion such as a wedding or a prom.
- **Style**. Choose two styles that describe your item from the drop down list.
- **Tags**. Just like your title, you want to load your tag section with keywords people will use to search for your item.

Obvious keywords are the style, color, size, use, etc. Try to use as many phrases as possible that describe your item or what it is used for – prom dress, wedding dress, linen table cloth, or custom made lace and satin prom dress. Put yourself in your buyer's shoes for a minute. What words would you use to search for your item? Etsy gives you thirteen tags. Use every one of them.

- **Materials**. Some people want to know what materials you used to make your item. You can list up to thirteen separate materials.
- **Price**. Enter your price here.
- **Quantity**. How many of this item do you have for sale?
- **Shipping**. Be sure to state your processing time, and the country your item is shipping from.

In the ships to section, you can set your pricing. Set your price for domestic shipping first.

If you plan on shipping internationally, the first box will let you ship anywhere in the world and set a price for that. If you only want to ship to certain countries, you can choose them from the drop-down box, and price shipping to each country individually.

When you set a shipping price, make sure you include the cost of boxes, envelopes, bubble wrap, labels, tape, and driving to and from the post office. You don't want to set your price so high as to discourage people from buying from you, but you should try to cover all your costs.

Another option is to offer free shipping and roll the cost of shipping into the price of your item.

Whatever you do, keep your shipping costs competitive with other sellers offering similar items.

- **Preview** your item. If everything looks good, go ahead and press enter to send your listing live.

That's it. You've listed your first item on Etsy. Once you have four or five listings under your belt, it will get quicker.

....

You now know how to set up your Etsy shop, list your items for sale, and how to discover items to sell and at what prices they are currently selling.

Get started today, and keep experimenting with new products and tweaking your Etsy shop. Success will follow your hard work.

KINDLE BOOK MARKETING

I**'ve been self-publishing Kindle books** for nearly two years now. It is one of the best ways to make money online.

It's also a lot of work.

A lot of the "Gurus" out there are marketing books and courses that label Kindle books as a good source of passive income. Trust me; **Kindle Income** is anything but passive. If you expect to keep the money rolling in, you need to be out there—constantly tinkering with this, and tweaking that. But, more on all that later.

One book normally isn't going to make you a whole lot of money. The real magic starts after you have eight to ten books in print.

SO HOW DO YOU GET STARTED?

First off you need a great idea.

- You need to produce a well-written book.
- You need to publish your book.
- Just because you published a book doesn't mean anybody's going to read it. You need to get the word out and help people find your book.
- The Kindle world has very few one book wonders. If you want to make money writing, the best advice I can give you

is as soon as you're done writing a book, get started writing your next book.

SUCCESSFUL BOOK IDEAS

Finding a book topic is a lot like shopping for a new car. You need to work at it to find the right one. For me, I need to try it on and make sure it's going to be a good fit for me. After all, I'm going to spend several months working on it. If I don't like the topic, chances are no one else will either.

Normally, I start out by brainstorming topics. I put together a list of twenty or thirty possible topics. Then I start to narrow it down a bit. When I've got my list down to three of four ideas, I explore them in more detail.

The first thing I do is type my idea into the Amazon search bar. It gives me a quick overview of what books are currently available on Amazon. How many books are similar to yours? How well they are selling, and how have different authors have approached the subject.

The nice thing about doing your initial research on Amazon is you can discover current books that are selling now. When you find one that sounds interesting, examine the description. If it has possibilities, kick the tires a bit. Amazon lets you read the first ten percent of most books so that you can check out the table of contents, the writing style, and some of the information offered inside.

Don't stop there. Read some of the reviews. Most of them will only be a line or two. They normally won't tell you much—maybe whether the writer liked the book, or not. Some of the longer reviews may go into detail about what they liked, or what they hated about it. Really-good reviewers will tell you what they wished would have been included in the book.

This is all gold. Use it to help shape your book into something readers want and are asking for. Keep your notebook handy. Take copious notes while you're doing your research.

Amazon also tells you how well books on your topic are selling. Midway down the book description page is a section titled "Product Details." It shows the books "Amazon Best Seller Ranking." If the book is ranked in a category, it will show you the ranking, and the category it is ranked in.

The lower the number, the better the book is selling. Most authors look for several books in a category to be ranked at 20,000 or lower. This means the book is selling four to six copies a day, which gives you a shot at making some decent money. A ranking of 50,000 means the book is probably selling one to two books a day. A ranking of 100,000 means the book is selling about one or two copies a week. A ranking above 500,000 tells you the book is gathering dust on Amazon's virtual shelves.

```
Product Details
File Size: 3810 KB
Print Length: 595 pages
Publisher: Ecco (September 18, 2012)
Publication Date: September 18, 2012
Sold by: HarperCollins Publishers
Language: English
ASIN: B008LV913M
Text-to-Speech: Not enabled
X-Ray: Enabled
Word Wise: Enabled
Lending: Not Enabled
Enhanced Typesetting: Enabled
Amazon Best Sellers Rank: #85 Paid in Kindle Store (See Top 100 Paid in Kindle Store)
    #1 in Kindle Store > Kindle eBooks > Biographies & Memoirs > Arts & Literature > Composers & Musicians
    #1 in Books > Arts & Photography > Music > Biographies > Country & Folk
    #1 in Kindle Store > Kindle eBooks > Biographies & Memoirs > Arts & Literature > Authors
```

Unless you've got a really great message or some startling discovery, you probably want to table an idea, if there aren't at least one or two books in the category that rank under 20,000.

YOU NEED TO PRODUCE A WELL-WRITTEN BOOK

You don't have to be another Stephen King or Amanda Hocking, but you do need to know how to turn a phrase.

If you write nonfiction people will be more forgiving of grammatical errors, as long as you give them the information you promised. If you're writing a novel, people expect to be entertained. You'd better be at the top of your game if you want to make big sales.

Keep in mind; no book is going to be perfect, especially on the first go around. Every book should go through several rounds of proofreading for grammatical errors and typos.

One of the fastest ways to get your book torn apart in the Kindle world is to publish a poorly written book, loaded with typos. It's going to put you on the fast track to bad reviews. Not only will it tank this book, but probably your next book, too.

If you're not up to the task of editing your book, ask a friend who is good with English. Another option is to hire a proofreader or copy editor on Fiverr or another freelancing site.

GET YOUR MANUSCRIPT READY FOR PUBLICATION

It's relatively easy to publish your book on Kindle.

I've read a lot of complicated descriptions about how to properly format your manuscript in HTML, or with this, or that eBook editing program. The truth is – you can do it just as well in MS Word.

Here are a few tips to help you tame your manuscript with Word.

- Set your page margins to six-inches times nine-inches.
- Don't paste your pictures into the text. Use Word's Insert picture function—it will ensure your pictures are displayed properly. Better yet, don't include pictures.
- Insert a page break after each section. Readers get a better reading experience by being able to start each new section on a fresh page.
- Stick with the basic fonts. Use Arial, Calibri, or Times Roman in either 11 or 12-point size type.
- Don't format your eBook like you would a print book. People are going to read your eBook on all sorts of different reading devices – Kindle, PC, Phone, and Tablets. Readers

can change the font and type style for most books. Just make sure your basic layout is good—everything else will work out.

- Add a clickable table of contents to your book. It'ss easier than it sounds and will make your book appear more professional. To get started: Go through your manuscript and highlight the chapter titles. After you highlight each chapter title, click on *Heading 1* in the *Home* section of the toolbar. Do this for each chapter. Next, highlight all your sub-headings, and select Heading style 2. This will differentiate them from the chapter titles when they appear in your table of contents.

The last step is to add your table of contents. Go to a blank page where you want to insert your table of contents. Click on the *References* tab in the upper toolbar. At the far left, you will see *Table of Contents*. Click on it. Select *Insert Table of Contents*. A little further down you're going to see a checkmark where it says, *Show Page Numbers*. Click on the box with the check mark to remove it. Click OK at the bottom of the page.

Only one step to go.

Type the words "Table of Contents" at the top of the page. Highlight it, and select *Insert Bookmark*. Type "toc" where it asks you to insert the *bookmark name*. Doing this tells Kindle your table of contents, and will make it available to readers as a menu option.

PUBLISH YOUR BOOK

There are a lot of options available to authors who want to self-publish their book. The more popular sites are Kindle, Barnes & Noble, Smashwords, Kobo, and iTunes.

My recommendation is to start with Kindle. You can test out other sites after you've got some sales under your belt.

The reason I recommend Kindle is they currently control over 65 percent of the eBook market. You're a writer. You might as well go where the readers are, right?

To get started on Kindle, click on the following link: https://kdp.amazon.com/self-publishing/signin

Follow the directions to sign up for a Kindle Direct Publishing account.

When you're ready to publish your book, select the option to *Add a New Title*.

The first option you are given is to *Enroll this book in KDP Select*. My suggestion is to check this box. KDP is an amazing way to promote your book on Amazon. What happens is: Every ninety days you are enrolled in KDP, Amazon helps you build your audience by allowing you to give away downloads of your book for five days. Two other options to help you sell books are Kindle Countdown Deals and Kindle Unlimited. We will talk more about them later in this chapter.

BOOK DESCRIPTION

Your description can make or break your book.

Some authors write very short descriptions. That's a waste of valuable real estate. Your description needs to tell people what your book is about. It should be informative, enticing, and written in the same style as your book.

You don't want to give away the farm, but you need to give readers a reason to click the buy button.

I like to start off by asking a question. Then I go into more detail. Some authors begin with a shocking fact, or startling statistic. Other writers begin their descriptions by showing portions of the reviews they've received.

There's no right or wrong way to write your book description.

Make it fit you, and your book. If your book is really short, and very little of it appears in the preview, you may want to include an excerpt in your description. Many successful authors post a complete table of contents in their book description. It's in the "look inside" preview, but who knows how many potential readers will take the time to check it out?

TARGET YOUR BOOK

You enter two key details here.

First, you need to select two categories for your book. When you select categories, make sure they're relevant to your book.

On any given day, Amazon has close to twenty million books listed for sale. Readers find new books using one of two methods. Either they type keywords into the search bar, or they browse categories. For your book to be found by browsers, it's crucial for your book to rank among the top 100 books in its category. Many readers stop searching after the first 20 books in a category.

So, the category you choose is going to play a big part in determining the success of your book.

Some authors suggest you should pick easy categories starting out to ensure your book will rank higher in search. They put their books in marginal categories that aren't the best fit for their title. I've always gone for the category I want to rank in. If my book is a Presidential biography, that's the category I choose. If my book is about selling on eBay, I choose the e-commerce category in business and computers. I want to rank up there with other big-name authors in my category.

If you're not sure which categories to list your book in, check the categories your closest competitors are listed in and go with those. Once your book has been out awhile, Amazon will slot your book into the categories it sells best in. You just need to get through the first few months.

The next thing you need to do is add keywords to help people find your book.

The keywords you choose are crucial to your book's success. The keywords I chose for this book are Kindle publishing, Etsy business, eBay business, eBay guidebook, how to sell on Amazon, how to sell on Fiverr, and how to self-publish on Kindle.

Notice, none of my keywords are single words. Think about how you search for a book. You might start with eBay, then move out to eBay profits, or online auction sales. Some experts suggest you should include the names of popular authors and book titles. The problem is doing that violates Amazon's terms of service, and could get your book pulled from the site.

As your book starts to sell, keep refining your keywords, until you get down to seven you feel will get the job done.

Remember, you can change keywords any time. If your book isn't selling—try changing up your keywords. Give them at least a week to see what happens. If you don't see an increase in sales, continue to tweak your keywords until you're happy with the results.

UPLOAD BOOK COVER AND BOOK FILE

Best advice you will ever get. No matter how good you think, you are, never—ever, design your book cover.

Here's a review one of my books received with a self-designed cover: "Got this during a free promo. No way I would have paid money for it with this cheesy cover, but it's actually a decent book."

Think about the last time you bought a book. One of two things caught your eye. Either the title or the cover. Maybe, a little bit of both.

A great cover doesn't need to be expensive. Sure, you can commission someone to create custom artwork and get a unique design out there. That can easily cost you $500, $1000, or more. I take a slightly different tack. I hire several different designers on Fiverr. This gives me several covers to choose from. I start out with the best one.

If sales aren't what I expect, I switch out my covers and see if it helps sales.

I'm writing this in mid-November. My eBay book sales have been sluggish for the last several months. One day I noticed several of the regular sellers in my category had switched out their covers, and were making some headway on the charts. I gave it a shot, too, and sure enough—it gave my titles a nice boost in sales.

PREVIEW YOUR BOOK

One of the things I always do is download a copy of my book to my Kindle Fire every few days as I'm writing it. That way I can read it in the format my readers are going to see it in.

This does two things:

- It forces me to read the book the way most of my readers will.
- It alerts me to any formatting errors so I can get them corrected before publication.

Whatever you do, don't publish your book with formatting errors. Readers will blast you with terrible reviews, and tank your book.

VERIFY RIGHTS AND SET PRICE

Before you publish your book, you need to verify your publishing rights. Normally, if you are the author of the work, you just click worldwide and let her rip. If there's a reason you can only publish your book in certain markets, select those areas, and you're ready to roll.

Pricing is a sensitive area for most authors. We all want to get as much money as we can for our books, but you need to balance that with what readers are willing to pay.

Amazon gives you some guidance based upon the royalties they pay.

- Books priced between 99 cents and $2.98 pay the author a 35 percent royalty.
- Books priced between $2.99 and $9.99 pay the author a 70 percent royalty.
- Books priced over $9.99, from $10.00 to $200.00 (the maximum amount you can charge on Kindle) pay a 35 percent royalty.

This tells us Amazon feels the sweet spot for Kindle book prices is somewhere between $2.99 and $9.99. We know this because this is where Amazon pays authors the highest royalties.

From my personal experience, books priced at $2.99 sell really well; at $3.99 you're going to encounter some resistance; depending upon how long your book is, and what the competition is charging. Your book may still sell okay at $4.99 and $5.99. Anything over $5.99, and you're going to hit some serious resistance unless you are a celebrity or a big-name author.

A lot of authors sell their books for 99-cents. That makes it tough to make any money. A 99-cent book pays 35-percent royalties. That means you make 35-cents for each copy sold. To make ten bucks, you need to sell thirty books, whereas, at $2.99, you only need to sell five books to make that same ten bucks.

That's not to say 99-cents is a bad pricing strategy. I use it when my sales are weak. Last month one of my titles ran out of steam. I priced it at 99-cents for three weeks to try and pick up some momentum. It sold 100 copies at 99-cents. Since I returned the price to $2.99, it is on course to sell sixty copies.

99¢ is also a viable launch strategy for your book. Smart authors slowly transition their prices after launch. The first week, or month, after their KDP Free run, they drop their book's price to 99¢. As they continue to gather momentum and reviews, they slowly increase their price to $1.99-$2.99-$3.99, etc. Contrast that with the way the New York Publishing houses do it. They price their titles at $1.99, or $2.99, for a day, or a week, then jump to $13.99 or $15.99. WTF! If an indie author did that, his book sales would shrivel up and die.

After you've entered your price, check the box at the bottom where it asks you to confirm rights, then click publish.

You'll be a published author in twelve hours or less.

I'VE PUBLISHED MY BOOK, NOW WHAT?

That's a good question.

The first thing you want to do is download a copy of your book, and read it over. Check for formatting issues, typos, and grammatical errors. This is your last chance to change things up before readers get a peek at it.

If you're happy with everything, schedule your free promo days (if you enrolled your book in KDP). Every author has a different strategy for this. My thought is five-days works the best for new authors. It gives you time to build momentum. Normally your first few days are going to be slow, but as time moves on people will start downloading more copies.

HOW TO GET REVIEWS

Another magical thing begins to happen on day three of your free giveaway. You start to get reviews. Amazon says you should average one review for every thousand copies downloaded, or sold. That means if you get 5,000 free downloads you can figure you will get five reviews. Sometimes you get more. Sometimes you can have a great giveaway and not get any reviews. Don't sweat it, it happens.

I was really worried about my first few books. Reviews were scarce, and all the experts said, "You can't sell books without reviews." I finally asked some friends to review my book. Some of them did, some didn't, but most of those reviews weren't very helpful. Friends tend to write one or two line reviews that go something like this, "A great read. I liked it."

The thing is readers like reviews that have a little meat to them. They want to know why the reviewer liked the book, or why they didn't like it. They want to know why the reviewer found your book useful or entertaining.

Don't worry. Those reviews will come. Four years, and nearly forty books later, I have over 600 reviews. A lot of them are really great four and five-star reviews, a few of them are one and two-star reviews. Good reviews happen. So, do bad reviews. All of them will help sell your books.

I've gotten to the point I only read one and two-star reviews. Many them are written by crackpots or grammar Nazis, but now and then you'll find a few gems. For the most part, the reason readers leave a bad review is they didn't like the writing style, or the book didn't contain the information they expected. Others say they liked it—but... (When you see reviews like this about your book take them seriously. Go back, and see if they're right. Could, or should, you have provided more information or covered alternate topics?

Reading your reviews is a great way to ensure your books are on topic, and providing the best information possible.)

KINDLE BOOK MARKETING 101

There's a lot of advice out there about how to market your book. I'm not a big believer in any of it.

I've sold thousands of books in the last year without doing anything other than optimizing my Amazon profile. So, what I'm going to do is show you how to maximize your profile on Amazon, then I will share a few tactics to help increase your book sales.

BOOK DESCRIPTION

Earlier when I discussed how to list your book on Kindle, I talked about book descriptions.

What you need to understand is your book description is a work in progress. You want to keep tweaking it. Test different versions, until you get the best description, you can.

Never be satisfied until you get the sales you want. Try writing a description of your book. Introduce your characters. Summarize your book. Lead with complimentary reviews.

You never know what's going to attract people's attention until you give it a shot.

If you think you've saturated the market in one category, tweak your description, so it appeals to a different group of buyers. If your reviews suggest some readers are looking for alternate information, do a quick revision—then target your book description towards them. I do this all the time, and normally it creates a nice boost in sales.

KINDLE COUNTDOWN DEALS

Amazon developed several marketing programs to help authors sell more books.

The first program is KDP Free Days. I already talked about them some earlier in this book. The way they work is if you enroll in KDP, every ninety days you can give your book away for five days, or you can run a Kindle Countdown Deal for seven days.

KDP free days can be used to launch a new book or to launch the career of an unknown writer. Amazon gives you five free days in every ninety day period. You can give your book away five days in a row, for five separate days, or for one two-day period, and one three-day period. How you choose to use them is entirely up to you.

If you do an internet search, you'll hear a lot of talk about how KDP Free Days don't work anymore. That may be true; it may not. It depends upon you, and upon your book. It's all about how you choose to market your book. There are still a lot of authors who've launched a successful book, or career using KDP Free Days.

Kindle Countdown Deals give authors a method to promote their books by lowering the price for a limited time.

For every ninety days your book is enrolled in KDP, you can run a Countdown Deal promo, or use KDP Free Days (not both). With the Countdown Deal, authors can promote their discounted prices for as little as one hour, up to seven days. You can choose to set your book's price at 99¢ for the entire promo, or you can set in on a sliding scale—where it moves up in price after a certain time-period. Discount pricing depends upon the regular price of your book.

Each time a reader clicks into your book description Amazon shows the promotional pricing beside a Countdown timer, so buyers know how much time is left on the offer. Amazon also has a special landing page set up for Countdown Deals so that readers can search for those books only.

Recently Amazon added another promo for authors enrolled in KDP. It's called Kindle Unlimited, and what it does is let subscribers read an unlimited number of books for only $9.99 per month. You get paid each time a reader selects your book. The more pages they read, the more money you make. The current rate paid to authors varies based upon how much money Amazon has stashed into their secret fund. (The November payment averaged 55¢ for each 100 pages read.)

Another program just made available to indie authors lets them set their books up for pre-order on Amazon. The neat thing with this program is all the sales go live on the day your book launches, so if you score enough pre-orders, you can rocket your book up the charts from Day 1.

AMAZON AUTHOR CENTRAL

Amazon created Author Central as an area for writers to showcase information about themselves and their books.

One thing we know, if people like your writing style, or message, they're going to want to know more about you—what you look like, how you got started writing, where you live, and what other books you've published.

To claim your Author Central page, visit the following link:

https://authorcentral.amazon.com/gp/home?ie=UTF8&pn=irid37437482

Add an author biography to introduce yourself. Make sure you include a picture. Readers want to know what you look like.

Author Central gives you a place to collect all your books in one place so readers can browse through them. Each time you publish a new book, be sure to click on Add Book, to add you latest title to your list of books.

Amazon offers the ability to link your blog and Twitter account to your Author Central Account. When you do this, your most recent tweet shows up, along with highlights from your three most recent blog posts. Talk about a great way to engage your readers and get them to follow you.

You also have a spot to upload book trailers or promotional videos. If you're photogenic, or good with video, you could create a whole series of videos so readers can learn more about you and your books.

A lot of authors link their books to Facebook or their author website, but a link to Author Central might pay off better over the long haul. Not only does it introduce readers to you, but it also gives you a great opportunity to sell more of your books.

FINAL THOUGHTS

Writing an eBook is a great way to make some extra money.

Don't let the hype fool you. One book isn't going to make you rich. Over time, if your book is well-written, and on a popular topic, it can bring you several hundred dollars per month in royalties.

The real magic starts when you have a backlist of ten to twenty books in a related field. When this happens, people will read one of your books. If they like it, chances are they will pick up one or two more. Some of them may even read all your books.

If you want to make money writing, look at each book as a stepping stone to a larger audience and increased sales.

Many authors insist a strong author platform is your best marketing tool.

Their thought is you need an author website, a blog, and at the minimum, a Facebook, and Twitter account. It depends on you, your style of communication, and how much time you have available to spend promoting your books.

Most recently, I've started to pay to play.

When I launch a new book, I run two or three promos to rev up sales. The first day, I run promos with [James H. Mayfield Book Promotions](#) and [bknights](#) on Fiverr. Those promotions get my book moving up the charts. On day two, I run another promotion on [freebooksy.com](#). Running multiple promotions is more expensive, but it usually helps me rank number one in my category for the remainder of my free book promotion. That assures maximum visibility among my potential readers.

The total cost for all three promotions is roughly $100.00—a small price to pay if sales take off.

BONUS EXCERPT 1 – SOCIAL MEDIA MARKETING MADE EASY

(Here's an excerpt from one of my newest books, **eBay Business Expert**. This section focuses on how to use Social Media, especially Facebook, to grow your business. You can check the entire book out by following this link, eBay Business Expert.)

Social Media Marketing for eBay Sellers

Do you need to blow up social media to sell on eBay and Amazon?

It's sort of like asking, are you a glass is half full, or a glass is half empty type of person. If you're a glass is half full type, you're going to scream "Damn right! You have to be on social media, because—that's where the people are." If you're a glass is half empty type you're going to piss and moan "what's the point? I'm selling my stuff on eBay, not on Facebook and Twitter."

You probably see where I'm going with this.

Online sellers are divided on the need for social media, its uses, and its outcomes. Some sellers will tell you they couldn't have gotten where they are without it; others will say "Why bother!" or "Hey! I tried it, and it didn't make any diff. My sales stayed the same."

I'm going to try not to take sides here. My goal is to give you the information you need to implement social media in your eBay business should you choose to do so.

My primary focus is going to be on Facebook, Twitter, and Pinterest because they are the three powerhouses behind social media today. Facebook and Twitter get a bigger mention because they are the go to social media sites. Pinterest gets a bigger mention because it is the one sellers say works best.

Does that mean you need to use all three? Or that you should focus exclusively on Pinterest because it's what works best for most sellers? No. It means you should start out slow. Pick one or two social media platforms and spend ten or fifteen minutes on them two or three days a week.

A PEW University study on social media usage provides one more relevant piece of information for savvy online marketers—over half of the people who visit social media sites are active on more than one site. For marketers the implication is clear if you want to reach your primary customer base, you need to be active on several social media platforms. Using one social media platform isn't going to cut it. Think a minimum of two, maybe even three social media platforms, if you want to reach your target audience effectively.

When you're first getting started, watch what other sellers in businesses like yours are doing on social media. Like some of their posts and start building your network. Make a few short posts. Put up a few pictures, or some short videos. Rinse and repeat.

The key to success with social media is to post regularly, comment when someone likes or comments on one of your posts, and keep a conversation going with your followers. Over time you will develop a following of your own.

Don't try to move too quickly, or fast-track your way to success. There are a lot of places on and off of eBay where you can purchase 500 or 1,000 likes. Don't be tempted. Phantom fans who don't comment on your posts, or like them, aren't going to do your business any good over the long haul.

Remember, it's not a contest to see who can get the most followers. It's all about getting the most followers who will engage with you on a regular basis, and who will share your content with their friends and followers.

That's how you build your business using social media. Give more than you get, share content your followers like, enjoy, and can use. If you do this, sales will follow.

Social Media by the Numbers

According to a PEW University study published in 2014, seventy-one percent of adults who use the Internet are on Facebook. Twitter, LinkedIn, Instagram, and Pinterest lag way behind with adult usage rates that fall somewhere between 23 to 28 percent.

Here are a few key takeaways for anyone planning to use social media to grow their online business.

- 31 percent of seniors are on Facebook.
- 53 percent of young adults age 18 to 29 are on Instagram. And, over half of these users visit the site daily.
- Women are three times more likely to use Pinterest than men. 42 percent of women who use the internet are on Pinterest, versus 13 percent of men.

If you need more help in choosing the correct social media platform to reach your key demographics, check out the rest of the PEW University study.

Facebook users are aging with a larger percentage of seniors over age sixty-five on the site. Women are more likely to frequent Facebook than men.

Twitter usage is higher among young adults ages eighteen to twenty-nine and falls off sharply among users at age forty-nine. Young adults and Afro-Americans are more likely to engage on Twitter.

Instagram has a high usage rate among young Americans ages eighteen to twenty-nine, and among Afro-Americans.

Pinterest users are primarily women, who tend to be college educated and more affluent.

LinkedIn is used less than other social media sites but could be helpful if you are marketing to individuals between the ages of fifty to sixty-five. LinkedIn users also tend to be college graduates, with a higher annual household income.

The PEW University study does leave out one important group—teenagers.

If you're marketing primarily to teens, you need to check out a 2014 study by Piper Jaffray ... <u>Taking Stock With Teens – Fall 2014</u>.

Here is some of the information you will discover.

- Your message better look good on an iPhone, because 67 percent of teenagers either have or plan on getting an iPhone.
- Instagram and Twitter are the social media sites most frequented by teens. So if teens are your target audience, you need to include more pictures, video, and music in your posts, and fewer words.
- Pinterest is the least used social media site among teens.
- Facebook is used by fifty percent of all teens but is not as popular as it was in the past.

Another important concept online sellers need to grasp is the people you want to reach, spend a large portion of their day online. Many of them rarely if ever leave social media sites, so if you don't engage with them there, you're not going to be able to sell to them—period.

Facebook

Facebook is the big kid on the block in social media marketing. It used to be the "in" site for kids, but now that it has gone mainstream Facebook has become the primary social media platform used by marketers to reach women, age thirty-five to sixty.

If you haven't checked your Facebook News Feed lately, one of the first things you'll notice is the changes in the content you see. Many of the top posts shown in your News Feed today are paid spots that Facebook considers relevant to your interests. Your friend's posts are still there, but they're intermixed with paid content Facebook thinks might grab your interest, and make them a few bucks to boot.

Something else you need to understand is the majority of Facebook users access the site only from mobile devices. This means you need to keep your posts short, with quick easy to load pictures and videos. You should also check out every post you make to ensure it looks good on an Android or IOS (Apple) device.

Getting started

Facebook is all about engaging with other users. That means your primary goal is to provide content that makes users want to like, comment on, and share your posts.

How do you do that?

Look at the popular posts in your News Feed, the one's users have liked and shared. The odds are they have at least one thing in common. Nine times out of ten they are visually oriented, which means they contain pictures or videos.

Facebook pictures come in a number of varieties, but they all share one common trait. They're of a person, or a cute furry pet—maybe even a baby. They're of a person making a funny face, or stuck in a strange place, or doing something unusual. Other times it's a picture of someone famous along with one of their quotes.

If you pay attention, you will see dozens of similar pictures in your News Feed every week. Some of them are cartoon images with catchy phrases; others are quotes from famous people. Many are product images with tag lines that scream out – "new from" … "on sale now" … "check out our new line of."

These types of images are a great way to catch people's attention and garner a bunch of quick likes and shares. The thing to remember when creating your items like these is to keep it legal. Don't just grab pictures you like off of the internet and add a snazzy quote. Make sure the image is copyright free. If you're in doubt, the best way to select a "legal" picture is to visit a clip art site and invest a few bucks in paying for one-time rights to use the image. Two such sites I use all the time are <u>Dollar Photo Club</u> and <u>Can Stock Photo</u>. Most of the images on these sites cost under five bucks, less if you buy multiple credits, and they're easy to manipulate using MS Paint so you can create awesome shareable images.

Videos are hot on social media, and if your video catches on it can go viral quickly and spread across the internet.

Make your videos tasteful and keep them focused on your product line. In my case, I sell old books and magazine articles. One video I include in all of my eBay listings is of Professor Puppet explaining my business and the types of items I sell. It helps people understand what my business is all about.

Other videos that would complement my product line would be reviews of historical books, how to videos about book and magazine collecting and special interest videos on historical events. Each of them would promote interest in the types of items I sell.

When I purchased my first Otterbox case, I couldn't figure out how to get it apart. Sure it came with a short set of directions in a smattering of different languages, but that wasn't enough to help me install the case. To get my phone inside of my new Otterbox case I had to search YouTube for a quick tutorial. (If you haven't discovered it, the trick to removing that thin outer shell is to slip a credit card underneath and pry it up. Thanks again, YouTube.)

A smart seller would have a similar video on his Facebook page, and in his eBay item listing. It's good customer service, and it's likely to be shared time and again bringing customers back to your eBay listing and Facebook page. *Tip: if you decide to include someone else's video or photo in your listings or on your blog or website—get permission first. Contrary to popular belief, most pictures and videos on the internet are copyrighted, so it is illegal to reproduce them without proper permission.*

If you sell men's, women's, or children's clothes every new season or product line you take on gives you the opportunity to add a new video to your Facebook page. If you're unsure how to do this, check out Lauren's Fab Finds for more ideas.

Create more effective Facebook posts

There is a whole lot of advice available about how to create more effective Facebook posts. Here's a short list that should help you boost audience engagement.

1. Keep your words to a minimum. Social media is constantly evolving, and the most effective posts are visually oriented.

If you want to maintain user engagement keep any text short—80 to 120 characters should be the max.
2. Don't link to stuff off of Facebook. Facebook users prefer to stay in their own little world.
3. Don't oversell. Facebook users are leery of marketing and are quick to steer away from sales pitches.
4. Don't post the same content on Facebook that you do on other social media sites. Your followers expect new and exciting content, not yesterday's news, or recycled post from Twitter or your blog. Don't disappoint them.

How to Sell on Facebook

All of this begs the question if people don't like to be sold to on Facebook, how do you get them to buy your stuff?

That's a good question, and one smart sellers are working hard to crack. The key is to understand what brings people to social media sites in the first place.

According to an April 2013, study published in The Atlantic the number one and three reason people go on social media sites is voyeurism. Facebook is the perfect tool to spy on your neighbors and friends. The catch is: Facebook users are consensual Peeking Tom's. We give each other permission to poke their noses into our back doors.

The number two reason people say they visit social media sites is to relieve boredom. They've got nothing better to do, so they turn to Facebook, Twitter, and similar sites to live vicariously through others.

And, the final reason given for visiting social media sites is to message between friends.

So, there you have it.

- Voyeurism
- Boredom

- Messaging

If you are using social media to reach these people you need to play to these needs.

Every post, picture, and video you place on social media sites need to take people behind the scenes and give them a sneak peek of what your business or industry is all about. Make it personal, make it entertaining, show vulnerability, and poke fun at yourself.

At the same time, you need to make sure your posts are engaging. Encourage communication with your social media followers, and schedule time every day to follow up with them. If someone comments on one of your posts, respond to them, even if it's just to say "thanks" or "hi."

If you do these things, your posts will play into the reasons people visit social media sites.

Basics of Facebook Marketing

Create a Facebook Fan Page. Don't use your personal Facebook page. It's unprofessional, and it doesn't give you all of the tools you need to engage with your followers.

It's easy to create a Facebook Fan Page. Go to https://www.facebook.com/pages/create.php.

That's going to bring up the following page where you select the category to place your Facebook Fan Page in.

The choices are:

1. Local Business or Place
2. Company, Organization or Institution
3. Brand or Product
4. Artist, Band, or Public Figure
5. Entertainment
6. Cause, or Community

Local Business or Place   Company, Organization or Institution   Brand or Product

Artist, Band or Public Figure   Entertainment   Cause or Community

Select the category that best describes your business. For most online sellers it's going to be local business or place, or brand or product, depending on how you're trying to promote yourself. If you're an author, artist or musician choose an artist, band, or public figure. It's pretty self-explanatory.

The next step is to set up your Facebook page and give it a name. Your page name should be a no-brainer. If you have a business name or eBay store name that should be the name of your Facebook page. Make it easy for buyers to find you.

Make sure to fill out the about section, and provide a link to your eBay store so people can easily find you. Add appropriate keywords in the about section. In my case, I sell historical collectibles so I would want to work in several of the following keywords, "vintage historical collectibles—magazine articles, prints, and advertisements." This will make it easier for search engines to locate your page, and for viewers to learn what you're all about.

Another neat feature you will find at the top of your page is the ability to *create a call to action button*. The button gives you some different choices including—shop now, contact us, use app, watch video, book now, sign up, or play game. If you're an online seller, I'd suggest using shop now and linking to your eBay store, and Sign up with a link to your email list sign up form. If you choose only one call to action, make it the sign-up form for your email list. It will give you the biggest bang for your buck over the long haul.

Create an amazing Timeline Cover Photo. This is the rectangular image at the top of your Facebook page. It needs to reach out and grab viewer's attention. It could be one large photo or a collage of smaller photos showing yourself, your employees, or the products you sell. It may also be a good idea to add a tagline, or your business name, to your Timeline Cover Photo.

It's one of the first things people see when they come to your Facebook page, so you want to do your best to make it stand out, and grab people's attention. With that said, here's my best advice—don't do it yourself. Hire a designer on Fiverr or Elance to put together a professional design for you.

You also need to create a profile photo. Some sellers use their logo; others use a photo of one of their better selling products. My suggestion is to use a selfie. Studies show people are more likely to engage with photos of people, so give them what they want. Flash a big smile. If your audience would enjoy a joke—stick your tongue out at them, or make a funny face. A lot of sellers get all fancied up and wear a suit or dress. That's okay, but my thought is you should present a more casual appearance. Dress like you normally would. It makes it easier for people to connect with you.

Now it's time to start adding your first posts.

It scares a lot of people, but it's one of the easiest parts of creating a Facebook page if you give it some thought. Think about yourself for a moment. What type of content do you enjoy engaging with on Facebook? Chances are you said—videos, pictures, and short, entertaining posts.

That's the type of content you need to give your fan page visitors.

Create a couple of short two to three-minute videos that explain your business, and talk about the products you sell; introduce your employees; interview a few of your customers, and let them say what they like about doing business with you. Post a few pictures of products you sell. Put up a humorous photo of your dog or cat playing with your computer or crawling out of a packing box. Post a picture of a hot new product you're getting ready to list.

The truth is there are all sorts of things you can post about. You just need to place yourself in your buyer's shoes and figure out what they'd like to know about your business or product line.

eBay Store Apps

There are some apps that let you place your eBay store on your Facebook fan page. Some are more feature filled or work better than others, so I'm giving you a list of apps you can explore.

Auction Items Facebook App
https://apps.facebook.com/auctionitems/. This one lets you put your eBay store in a tab on your Facebook fan page. They also have apps available for Etsy and Bonanza store owners.

Easy Social Shop App
http://www.easysocialshop.com/ebay-facebook-shop/. It's a free and easy solution to get started selling on eBay.

StoreYa
http://www.storeya.com/ebay-to-facebook. StoreYa places a tab on your Facebook fan page so you can begin selling immediately. They also have apps that support Shopify, Amazon, Magneto, and WordPress among others.

3D Sellers
http://apps.ebay.com/selling?ViewEAppDetails&stab=3&appType=1&appId=SocialStore.3dsellers.com. Social Store from 3D Sellers is available in the eBay apps center and lets you add your eBay store to your Facebook fan page.

Boost your Facebook Post

Sometimes your Facebook posts need a little more oomph to reach more viewers.

I know what you're thinking. "Hey! I'm on Facebook because it's free. What do you mean I have to spend money to get my posts seen?"

I know, it's crazy, but it's true. Facebook has created a new way to make money, and part of it involves hiding your posts, or as they would have it—strategically placing them towards the top of a user's News Feed if you kick in a minor contribution to Zuckerberg and Company.

Here's what Facebook says about boosting your post. Boosted posts appear higher in your News Feed, so there's a better chance you will see them.

You can boost any post—video, picture, or text. To boost a post, click on Boost post in the lower left-hand corner of the post. After you do that, select the audience demographics you want to see your post, your budget, and the length of time to boost the post.

Pretty simple so far, right?

In most cases, five to fifteen dollars should get you a big enough boost to reach your audience. If it's something special, like a new product launch, maybe budget forty or fifty dollars. As for the audience, try to narrow the focus to your prime demographic. If it's showing your message is targeted to millions of readers try to narrow it down some. Shoot for something in the range of fifty to one hundred thousand for your target audience. For your time frame, you have a choice of one to seven days. If you boost it longer than two or three days you're going to find yourself pushing old news.

Create a Facebook Event to Promote Your Sale

A Facebook event may or may not work for you. The reason I say this is you can only create an event from your personal Facebook page, not from your Facebook fan page.

Don't get discouraged yet.

Promoting an event to your regular Facebook friends can help you introduce a new product line, or try out new ideas you normally wouldn't use with your regular customers.

Think of your event as a marketing test? It's a chance for you to try new things, and for your friends to get a hell of a deal. Promote it to them that way, and it will be a win-win situation for both of you.

If you're unfamiliar with Facebook events, the easiest way to think of it is as an online party invite. I've received them for family reunions, book launch events, and birthday parties. The great thing about creating a Facebook event is once you set it up, Facebook does all the work for you. It sends out the invites, collects RSVPs, and posts a reminder on the Facebook homepage for everyone who was invited.

The other cool thing is a Facebook event is super easy to create and manage. Here's a link to Facebook's instructions for creating an event.

Final takeaway

Facebook can be a great way to help grow your business. Like anything else it can become a bottomless pit sucking up all of your time if you're not careful.

To be successful selling on Facebook, you need to

1. Have a plan. Know what you want to accomplish. Do you want to make more sales? Encourage email sign ups? Engage more with customers?
2. Budget 15 to 20 minutes a day three or four days a week and stick to that time limit.
3. Be visual. Facebook users respond best to videos and pictures. Give them what they want, and you will be more successful.
4. Don't over-post, or under-post. If you post too often, users are going to unfollow you or turn off your News Feed. If you don't post often enough, people are going to forget who you are. Three to five good posts a week is enough to get your message out there.
5. Spend a few bucks to boost your posts, especially when you're first getting started. It will help you build your audience faster.

BONUS EXCERPT 2 – BOOKKEEPING MADE EASY

(Here's an excerpt from one of my book, **eBay Bookkeeping Made Easy**. This section shows online sellers how to manage your sales, profits, expenses, and cash flow using GoDaddy Accounting. You can check the entire book out by following this link, eBay Bookkeeping Made Easy.)

GoDaddy Bookkeeping is available as an app you can download from eBay's applications bar. Amazon and Etsy sellers can check out the online version by visiting this link http://www.godaddy.com/accounting/accounting-software.aspx?isc=gooob012&ci=87249.

The service was originally known as Outright and was taken over by GoDaddy last year. It's an online accounting solution that will serve the needs of most users. It automatically imports transaction data from your PayPal account and posts it to the proper categories. Users can also sync their business credit cards and checking accounts with the service.

For sellers conducting business on multiple platforms, GoDaddy Bookkeeping can import transaction data from eBay, Amazon, and Etsy. It also works with several invoicing services including FreshBooks, Shoeboxed, and Harvest.

Here's the least you need to know. GoDaddy Bookkeeping is available on the *Applications* tab on your *My eBay* page. Hover your mouse over *Applications* until it shows Manage Applications, click on this and scroll through the list of applications until you come to

Outright. Click on *Outright*, and select *Try It Free*. *(GoDaddy discontinued all free accounts as of December 21, 2014)*

GoDaddy Bookkeeping is available as a monthly ($9.99) or yearly ($99.00) subscription. Choose your poison and follow the prompts to get started.

Overview

The first page you see is your account overview. It contains all the basic information about your account. In the upper right corner, it shows your yearly profit or loss so you can tell at a glance where you stand. Below this is a graph that charts your income and expenses, a pie chart that shows your current month's expenses, and then a list of open invoices.

Below this is a section that shows Invoice Activity. Most online sellers aren't going to use this feature as all your invoicing is done through eBay, Amazon, Etsy, and your e-commerce storefronts. If you're running a side business where your customers pay through PayPal, this is where you would bill your customers for products or services sold.

In the left-hand column, you'll see four small blue boxes. The first box is labeled *New This Week* and tracks your new sales and any uncategorized expenses. To view your new transactions or uncategorized expenses click on the number, and it will take you to your general ledger.

The *Money I Have Box* lets you view the balances in your accounts – PayPal, Amazon, and any bank accounts you have connected.

The Money I Owe box shows your liabilities or the money you owe. Some of the accounts shown here are your eBay balance, and money owed to Amazon and Etsy for seller fees.

The last box is labeled *Taxes*. It shows you several key tax indicators for your business. The first line shows your estimated quarterly tax payment, and when it is due. The mileage line shows your year to date mileage expenses. When you click on mileage, it takes you to your general ledger and lets you log your mileage. The last line shows your *Sales Tax Liability*, so you always know how much you owe.

Below the four blue boxes, you should see two blue bars. *Add Account* lets you add your various seller accounts, PayPal Account, and any bank accounts you want to tie into GoDaddy Bookkeeping. *Refresh All* imports data from your connected accounts so that you're viewing the most recent information available.

If you scroll back up to the top of the page, you'll see your six control tabs – Overview, Income, Expenses, Reports, Taxes, and Manage. When you click on any of these they, open more program options.

Before I describe the control tabs, there's one other item I should cover. Sometimes a tan bar will appear just below the control tab. It shows program alerts or problems GoDaddy Bookkeeping may be experiencing with your account. When you click on the Fix It highlight, it will walk you through solving the problem so you can get your program up and running correctly again.

....

You can view your profit & loss statement anytime by clicking on the *view details* tab underneath where it says *(Year) Profit & Loss* on the GoDaddy Bookkeeping *Overview* page.

Your Profit & Loss statement gives you a quick overview of the financial health of your business. The top section shows your sources of income, and the bottom section details your expenses. The final line shows your "bottom line," or the actual profit or loss your business is making.

The default view for your P & L is the previous twelve months, but you have the option to change that any time you'd like. Scroll up to the top of the page under *Profit & Loss* where you see *ending*. You can choose the ending month or year, or you can change the time-period today, week, month, quarter, or year. To return to the chart select the chart icon on the right-hand side.

If you want to take a closer look at a transaction, all the items on your P & L are clickable. Select the one you want to examine, and it will take you to the general ledger page for that category.

Moving back down to the bottom of the page there are two tabs on the far-right side. Export lets you transfer P & L information to a Microsoft Excel file. Selecting print will give you a hard copy of your P & L.

Income

The income tab lets you manage your online income accounts. When you click on income, it takes you to your general ledger page for income, and you can view your most recent transactions.

Once again, all the transactions displayed are clickable. If you want to edit a transaction, select it, and make the needed corrections.

What I recommend here is to set up categories for all your income transactions so you can track where your money is coming from. When GoDaddy Bookkeeping imports income transactions, it brings all of them in under the general "sales" heading. If you're just selling on one venue, such as eBay or Amazon, that's not a problem. If you sell across multiple platforms, it's important to know what source your money is coming from. This way you can take corrective action if a sales venue is underperforming.

Every time you make a sale, GoDaddy Bookkeeping records it as two separate transactions. The merchandise portion is recorded under the "Sales" heading. If postage was charged on the transaction, it is recorded under the heading "shipping income."

If you want to add additional sales categories, select a transaction, and then scroll down the page until you see a heading labeled *Good to Know*. Over to the right-hand side, you will see a link labeled *Manage Categories*. Select it. This shows you a chart of your current income categories. To add a category, select *New Income Category*. Categorize it as *Business* or *Nonbusiness*, and then name the new category. After doing this, you need to select a tax category. To tie the category you created to sales; you would choose *gross receipts or sales*. Select *create*, and your new category is ready to use.

To give you an idea about how to use this, I added the following categories to my income account – eBay sales, Amazon, Bonanza, *eBid*, bidStart, Kindle, Create Space, and Audible. By doing this, I can keep separate tabs on each of my sales channels. It gives me better control over my business and allows me to spot patterns early as they're beginning to emerge.

After you set up your income categories, you need to assign each transaction to the proper category. The easiest way to do this is from the Overview page. Select *view details* to see your P & L. Click on *sales* in the income section of your P & L. This will pull up all your unassigned items. Select each item separately, and assign it to the proper income account. This step is pretty straightforward and should take just a few moments every day.

Whenever you're working on your P & L, you should also examine your uncategorized expenses. They're listed at the bottom of the P & L, just before you see your bottom line. Most items are categorized when they're imported, but there are usually a few uncategorized items, either because you purchased from a new supplier and GoDaddy Bookkeeping doesn't know how to classify it, or because the items you purchased from that supplier may fit into several different expense categories. Click on the individual unclassified transactions and assign them to the proper category.

If you do this every time you open your program, it will only take a few minutes of your time, and it will ensure your P & L is up-to-date and accurate.

Expenses

When you select expenses, it brings up the general ledger view for your business expenses.

You can set up personalized categories to customize GoDaddy Bookkeeping for your business needs. Select an individual expense to enter the edit mode. Scroll down the page until you see the heading *Good to Know*. Move your mouse to the far right of the page and click on *manage categories*. Select *new expense category* and follow the prompts. Categorize the expense as a business or nonbusiness expense and name it. Scroll through the *tax category list* to tie your new expense to the proper category, and then select *Create*.

I would suggest setting up custom categories for your internet and cell phone providers, storage space rental, etc.

I find it useful to lump a few expense categories together. The main category I do this with is postage. I throw all my shipping expenses in there – boxes, packing tape, stay free mailers, peanuts, you name it. The reason I do this is it makes it easier to compare my shipping expenses and shipping income. If my shipping income is equal to, or more, than my shipping expense, I know I'm on the right track. When they get out of whack, it's time for an intervention to determine what went wrong.

With my other expenses, my main concern is that they're consistent from month-to-month. If one month is way up without a similar bump in sales, it's time to investigate what happened. Sometimes it's a special purchase I had the opportunity to make; sometimes a number was entered wrong. The key thing is to watch your numbers and react quickly when you see that something is out of whack.

Reports

When you select reports, it brings you to your Profit and loss statement. GoDaddy Bookkeeping always shows you the chart first. Select *view as a table* to see your P & L Statement.

If you're running a business, you should know these numbers forwards and backward. Growth is good, but I like to see consistent numbers across the board.

When I'm comparing my book sales numbers, the first thing I do is compare them with the last few months. If sales seem unusually low, I examine last year's numbers to see if it's a seasonal trend. You should do the same thing.

Online sales are always slower in summer. They normally pick up by late August and run strong through spring. February and October can be iffy – they can go either way. The first half of

November can be the same way, waiting for Christmas buying to kick in.

Key point: Use your P & L to help forecast fluctuations in your business. Study it for trends, where sales are increasing or decreasing, or where expenses are rising. Put on your detective hat and figure out what's happening. Doing this will make you a better business person, and help your business to grow stronger over the long haul.

Taxes

The taxes section helps you with three specific areas.

- It provides your Schedule C information to make tax time a breeze. Just transfer over the numbers, and you're ready to file. Keep in mind; you're still going to need a tax advisor, or a good tax program, like TurboTax Business, or HR Block Business. GoDaddy Bookkeeping doesn't figure the home office deduction, tax credits, etc. They just provide you with the raw numbers to fill out your Schedule C.
- GoDaddy tracks your sales taxes due, so it's easy to file and submit your state reports. If you have eBay, Amazon, and Etsy set up to collect sales tax in your state, GoDaddy Bookkeeping will track all the information for you.
- Every time you log into your account, you can see your estimated tax payments and the date they are due. This way the due date and the amount you owe won't sneak up on you.

Manage

When you select manage, it displays a list of all the accounts you have connected to GoDaddy Bookkeeping. If any of the accounts have errors, you will see a tan bar displayed by them. Click on the blue *Fix It* link to take care of account issues.

If you want to connect more accounts, select *Add an Account* at the top of the page

....

Good to know

You can easily reassign categories if something is categorized incorrectly.

Most often when this happens, it's because the program does not recognize how to classify the transaction. To fix the problem select the item that needs to be classified. At the far right, it will say uncategorized item, select the correct category from the drop-down box, and press save.

You will also need to re-categorize items when you make a non-business related purchase. GoDaddy Bookkeeping has a *personal expense* category you can assign the item to so it is removed from your business records. If you sell a personal item and receive payment for an item through your PayPal account, you can reassign it to the *personal income* category.

Best advice

Keep a close eye on your accounting program. Update it every few days. It's easier to catch errors when just a few items are displayed. If you let it go too long, a large list of items to re-categorize can seem overwhelming.

BONUS EXCERPT 3 – EBAY SHIPPING TOOLS MADE EASY

(Here's an excerpt from one of my book, **eBay Shipping Simplified**. This section focuses on how to ship your items using the tools built into eBay and PayPal. You can check the entire book out by following this link, eBay Shipping Simplified.)

Both eBay and PayPal allow sellers to print shipping labels directly from their sites. The process is easy to use and allows you to print professional looking labels and invoices to include with your shipments.

Print eBay Shipping Labels

The easiest way to print shipping labels using eBay is to go into your *Selling Manager*. In the left hand, column find where it says *Selling Manager Pro*. Just down from there, you'll see the word *sold*. Select it.

That's going to bring up a list of your sold items. Locate the item you want to ship, and scroll over to the far-right column labeled actions. The first thing you should see is *Print Shipping*.

When you select *Print Shipping,* it takes you to the eBay ship your item page. When you click on it, the page is prepopulated with all your item information.

At the top of the page, you're shown the item description; the price paid, shipping fee, shipping service paid for, and the expected delivery date. The left-hand column contains the shipping information—the buyer's address and your address. If you need to make a change to either address, select change, and enter the correct shipping information.

Just below the address details, you'll see a box labeled Add a message to buyer email. I have a standard thank you message in here, but you can use it to tell your buyer a little more about the item or direct them to your store specials. It's up to you.

The center column contains the package details. It's where you choose the carrier, add shipping options, and choose your mailing date. eBay has two approved carriers the United States Postal Service (USPS), and FedEx. My shipping experience has all been with the USPS, so that's what I'm going to cover here. If you ship using FedEx, select them as the carrier and follow the prompts to complete your shipment.

The first thing you need to do is select your carrier. In this case, choose USPS.

Use the next box to select your shipping service. The choices are priority mail, first class package, parcel select, media mail, and priority mail express. The priority mail and priority mail express options let you select the level of service you want.

After you've selected your service, you have the option of printing the auction number, or some other message on the label. If you want to do this, check the box and type in your message. The default message is the auction id.

The final box lets you choose the mailing date. You can choose today, tomorrow, or the next day. The reason for this is you're supposed to mail your package the same day you print the label, so if you're printing the label today, but not mailing your package for two days, you should change the date. I've never had a problem with the post office if I'm a day or two late dropping the package in the mail, but now you know the correct way to do it.

The third column shows your postage cost broken down by the postage cost, the delivery confirmation fee, and the total cost. Below that, you have the option to hide the shipping so buyers can't see how much actual shipping cost you. It's your choice—if you're playing by the rules and charging actual shipping, let your buyers see the shipping cost. It will prove you're on the up-and-up.

When you're done, click purchase postage. When you do this, your PayPal account will be charged for the shipping fees. The next screen will show a mockup of the label. You can print a sample, or print the label.

After the label is printed, the program will automatically transfer tracking information into the item listing so buyers can follow the movement of their package as it is being shipped to them.

Alternatively, you can print your postage labels directly from PayPal. To get started open your PayPal account and locate the transaction you want to print the postage for. Click on the text where it says *Print shipping label*. It brings up the same shipping page we used above, so you can follow through using those directions.

Do I Need Insurance?

When eBay allowed sellers to charge customers for insurance, I required all my buyers to purchase it. It saved a lot of hassles. If the item was lost, the customer was taken care of.

What I discovered after shipping over 30,000 items is very few items were ever lost, stolen, or damaged in transit. I think I've had two damaged packages, and three lost packages in fifteen years. So, is insurance necessary? It depends on you, and your tolerance for loss. Most of the items I ship cost between twenty to twenty-five dollars. Insurance costs close to two bucks for each package. Take two bucks times thirty thousand packages, and that's close to sixty thousand dollars.

My losses in all this time have amounted to under one hundred bucks. If I'd bought insurance on every item, I shipped I'd be out close to $60,000. When you look at it that way—insuring my packages doesn't make sense.

But…insuring my more expensive packages does make me feel all warm and fuzzy inside. Because of that, I decided to pick a number where I would insure my shipments. If the value exceeds that number, I purchase insurance. For me, the magic number is fifty dollars. For you, it may be ten dollars or one hundred dollars. The best I can tell you is to choose your threshold for loss, then insure all shipments that exceed that number—that way you can sleep nights.

Several years ago, eBay introduced their Global Shipping Program. It's an easy way for sellers to jump into international selling without having to worry about shipping rules, customs forms, etc.

If you've been itching to get started with international sales, but were afraid of the extra work involved I suggest giving it a shot using eBay's Global Shipping Program.

Many small sellers are terrified of international shipping. They've heard so many horror stories; they're scared to give it a shot. They don't want to fill out customs forms or worry about whether their package is going to make it all the way to Timbuktu or not.

eBay has eliminated all the grief for sellers who use their Global Shipping Program. Sellers list their items just like they normally would. When their item sells, they ship it to an eBay shipping center in the United States.

Bing-Badda-Boom! As soon as it arrives at the shipping center, your responsibility for the shipment is over. From that point on eBay and their shipping partners assume all responsibility for getting your package to its destination.

Here's how it works.

When you list your item for sale on eBay, check the box to include your item in the Global Shipping Program, and you're good to go.

Some categories don't qualify for inclusion in the Global Shipping Program. When you bump into these, eBay will flag the item and let you know. I do a lot of selling in the collectibles category. Collectibles manufactured before 1899 don't qualify, so I see this issue pop up quite often. The only way around it is to ship the item internationally yourself. I'll discuss this option in more detail later.

When an item sells using the Global Shipping Program sellers can't send the buyer an invoice. eBay takes care of all this for you.

The reason is you have no way of knowing what their shipping fee will be.

Once the customer pays, you will receive your payment notice along with the address to ship your item to. An easy way to recognize a payment made through the Global Shipping Program is the address will include a long reference number.

Ship your item like you normally would. Include delivery confirmation, so you can be sure the item was received at the shipping center. Once you have confirmation the item was received, your part in the transaction is complete.

eBay's shipping partner—Pitney Bowes—will readdress the item, fill out all the appropriate customs forms, and ensure your item is delivered to the customer.

That's the way it should happen. Now and then things don't work out as planned—the customer doesn't receive the item, or it arrives damaged. As a seller, you're supposed to be protected from receiving negative feedback in such a situation. That's true to a point. You need to keep an eye on your feedback profile and keep after eBay to update it when errors are made.

I received a negative feedback due to a customer not receiving their item. I knew it wasn't received because that's what the seller wrote in his feedback. So, I called eBay customer service and explained the problem. After about fifteen minutes of researching the problem, the rep agreed I was not responsible. He removed the negative feedback while we were still on the phone.

If you experience a similar problem, contact eBay customer service immediately. When you call, have the listing item number and the feedback information available and ready to share with them. Make it easy for eBay to help you.

Overall the Global Shipping Program is a great way to increase your sales. During my peak selling period, international sales accounted for roughly thirty-five to forty percent of my eBay sales and profits.

If you're looking for an effortless method to grow your sales, opt into the Global Shipping Program and give it a shot.

Enable Items for International Shipping

We've already talked about eBay's Global Shipping Program and how easy it is to use, so why would anybody want to ship international packages on their own?

That's a great question.

It comes down to having more control over your shipping options, and the ability to make more sales. When you use eBay's Global Shipping Program, they figure in custom's fees, a markup to pay themselves and their shipping partner an additional profit, plus actual shipping costs. The final number eBay shows your customer for shipping can be mind-boggling and can cost you the sale.

Let me use the products I sell as an example. When I ship items internationally on my own, I charge $5.00 to ship items to Canada, and $9.00 for shipping anywhere else in the world. Sometimes I make a few extra bucks; sometimes I lose a few bucks, but over time it averages out. Keep in mind; the buyer is still on the line for duty and customs fees when their item arrives.

When I use eBay's Global Shipping Program, they charge my customer in the low twenty-dollar range for Canada, and in the low thirty-dollar range for Europe and the rest of the world. My items normally sell for sixteen to twenty-five dollars, so customers are confronted with some serious sticker shock when they're hit with eBay's shipping price.

Self-preservation is one of the major reasons I ship most international packages myself.

What I'm going to do now is walk you through setting up the international portion of your eBay sell your item form. It's structured the same way you set-up your domestic shipping options, so it should be easy to follow along and use.

....

Everything you need to set your international shipping options can be found in the box labeled *International Shipping*.

The first choice you are offered is to opt into the Global Shipping Program. In this case, you want to leave that box unchecked.

Below this, you have a drop-down box that offers you the option to select flat rate, calculated shipping, or no additional options. As a quick review, flat rate shipping is where you have one set shipping fee for all buyers; calculated shipping uses the eBay shipping calculator to determine the shipping price based upon where you are shipping your item to. The difference is—flat rate shipping is easier to set up and use, but calculated shipping can give buyers closer to you a break in shipping costs thus giving you the opportunity to grab additional sales from price conscious buyers.

After you choose your shipping method, you'll see another drop down box that says shipping. It gives you three choices: worldwide, chose a custom location, or Canada. I normally set up a separate price for worldwide and Canada—any more is overkill in my book. However, if you ship a lot of packages to Mexico, the UK or wherever go ahead and set up a special price for them too. The drop down box next to this lets you choose the type of service you wish to offer, and the box to the right of that lets you set your shipping price.

Below this, you see a line labeled *offer additional service*. You can use this to offer to ship to an additional location or to offer a different delivery method.

In the *additional ship to locations,* you can check off areas you are willing to ship to, and the buyer can contact you for more details. Some sellers have lots of rules about where they will, and will not ship too. Many sellers mark Malaysia, Italy, Mexico, Russia, etc. off limits because it's all over the internet other people have experienced problems when they ship packages there. In my book, that's all talk. I've shipped items to all those countries and never had a problem. All I'm saying is if you're going to put certain areas off limits, or discourage buyers from certain regions, wait until you have a problem with the area, then evaluate the situation to determine how you want to handle it.

The final line—combined shipping discounts, lets you apply your discount rules to this purchase if you set them up. My items are light and only add a few ounces to the package. Therefore I ship all additional items for free. It's a great way to encourage buyers to continue shopping with you. If you can't offer to ship all additional items for free—consider offering some type of discounted shipping for additional purchases. It will bring you more business over the long haul.

That's it. You're open for international business. Sit back, and wait for the orders to roll in.

I'm going to make one additional suggestion here. Take a few moments to help set buyer expectations. International buyers are like domestic buyers—they want to purchase their items today and receive them yesterday.

Most times, shipping goes smoothly, and items arrive on time, but there are many circumstances beyond your control, especially when you're dealing with international customers.

I normally post the following information in each of my listings and include it again in my shipping emails.

"Normal international delivery time is eight to fifteen business days, but it can often take four to six weeks—depending on customs, and other shipping issues. Please be patient, and take this into consideration when placing your orders."

It helps to set buyer expectations before the order is placed. That way if the customer asks where their item is you can refer them back to the info posted in your listing. By giving realistic delivery time frames up front, you're going to save yourself a lot of grief and wasted emails trying to explain why customers haven't received their packages yet.

Remember—International customers have you over the barrel. Tracking is virtually nonexistent for international shipments. The post office is experimenting with international delivery confirmation to select countries, but the service is spotty at best. There's no guarantee the mailman in Canada, or the UK, will scan your package when he drops it off. He may be having a bad day. He may be trying to outrun a dog. If your customer decides to file an item not received case, you're going to lose, because there's no way to provide proof of delivery.

Sorry to be the one to break it to you, but it's a fact of life when you're doing business on eBay. I've only had this happen once. A buyer in Germany opened an item not received case two days after paying for his item. There was no possible way it could travel from Iowa to Germany in two days.

Guess what? It didn't matter. eBay and PayPal decided the case against me because I didn't have proof of delivery. Like I said, this happened one time out of five thousand, so it's not a big deal.

One other quick comment here—many sellers assume proof of shipping is enough to win an international case. It's not. A stamped customs form from your post office is of no help to you if the buyer files an item not received case. If you can't show proof your item was delivered, you don't have a leg to stand on.

BONUS EXCERPT 4 – 25 TIPS & TRICKS TO BOOST YOUR SALES

(Here's an excerpt from my book, **eBay Ninja Tips & Tricks**. This section provides 25 tips and tricks any online seller can use to grow your business and increase your profitability. You can check the entire book out by following this link, eBay Ninja Tips & Tricks.)

Here are some tips to help you sell more, work faster, and make more money. Some are simple ideas you can use from day one, others will make more sense as you scale and grow your eBay business.

1) Set up a basic accounting system from day one. Your eBay life will run a lot smoother if you have a bookkeeping system in place from day one. It doesn't have to be anything sophisticated, just a simple way to record all your sales and expenditures. That way when tax time comes around, you have all the information you need close at hand.

My first bookkeeping system was a simple Excel spreadsheet. I used it to track my purchases, sales, and profits. I printed off all my PayPal receipts and stored them in a three-ring binder.

As time went by I transitioned to *QuickBooks*, and then to *Go Daddy Bookkeeping*. Each of these solutions made the process simpler by automating my everyday accounting tasks.

Take some time now to set up your accounting system.)See Bonus Excerpt number two for more information on using GoDaddy Bookkeeping to keep track of your sales and profits.)

2) Automate your feedback. Several apps will let you post feedback as soon as a buyer pays for your items. I use to think it was important to leave all my feedback personally, but when I started selling 700 to 800 items per month leaving feedback became a burden.

3) Use eBay's shipping tools. Shipping can easily become one of the biggest time sucks for eBay sellers. When you use eBay's shipping service, it automatically transfers addresses and other information over to the labels it prints. Most shipping options also offer free or discounted tracking on your packages, plus they transfer the tracking info directly into the listing so that buyers can check the progress of their shipments. As a result, you will get fewer questions to answer about when customers are going to receive their shipment.

(See Bonus Excerpt 3 for more information on how to use eBay and PayPal shipping tools. It also gives a brief tutorial on International shipping with eBay's Global Shipping program.)

4) Use free packing materials from the USPS. If you ship by priority mail, get your boxes and envelopes free from the post office. They will even deliver them to you for free.

5) Stop going to the post office. If you're shipping by priority mail, the post office will pick up your packages. You can schedule delivery by following this link

https://tools.usps.com/go/ScheduleAPickupAction!input.action

6) Take advantage of free listing days. eBay offers free listing promotions every month. Take advantage of as many of them as you can to save on fees.

Do the math before you list, or relist any items.

Sometimes you may need to let your items sit for a week or so while you wait for the next special to roll around.

(Note: 12/01/2016 – eBay has scaled way back on free listing promotions since I first wrote this. Occasionally you can still snag a free listing promotion for 500 or 1000 free auction listings, but they are few and far between compared to what they used to be.)

7) Offer free shipping. If it makes sense, offer free shipping on your items. eBay loves free shipping and will promote your items more often when you offer free shipping.

8) Offer a combined shipping discount. If offering free shipping doesn't work for what you sell, consider offering a combined shipping discount to buyers who purchase more than one item. You'd be surprised how many buyers will pick up another item or two when they can get free or discounted shipping on the additional items.

9) Respond quickly to buyer inquiries. Answer questions as quickly as you can. Potential buyers will lose interest if you make them wait too long for an answer. Unhappy customers will be delighted if you answer quickly, and let them know you're eager to help them solve their problem.

When you respond to customers—be positive. Thank them for writing you, and let them know it is a really great item. If a potential buyer wants to know something about your item, give them a little more information than they asked expected. Build extra-value into every item you sell.

Suppose a customer asks about the battery life on your iPad. Tell them, "It's a really nice iPad, with hardly any signs of wear. I mainly used it between classes. The only reason I'm getting rid of it is my parents gave me a new iPad Air for my birthday. The battery lasts about ten hours if you're just listening to music or surfing the web."

The extra information may tip the scales and help them decide to buy your item.

If it's a buyer who's unhappy with a recent purchase, let them know you're there to help, and that you understand their frustration. "Thank you for contacting me about your recent purchase. I'm very sorry to hear that you are unhappy with your item. I'll be glad to do whatever I can to make it right for you. Here are a few tips that may help…"

Say thank you often as often as possible. Offer to resolve any problems the buyer may have. If it's a potential customer, and they're on the line about whether the item will work for their intended use, or about the condition, I make sure to mention my 100 percent money back guarantee. That takes all the risk out of purchasing my item.

10) Sell International. eBay has a new Global Shipping Program that makes shipping internationally as easy as shipping in the United States. The way it works is you opt into the program when you list your item. When the item sells, eBay collects shipping, fees, and customs duties from your customer. Once your customer pays, eBay provides the address to their fulfillment center. As soon as they receive your package, your part in the transaction is complete.

From this point on eBay readdresses the package, and forwards it to your customer. They fill out all the customs forms, choose the right shippers, and complete all the heavy lifting for you.

If you haven't opted into the Global Shipping Program yet, give it a shot. Once I started selling internationally, sales jumped thirty to thirty-five percent.

11) Setup your customer FAQ. Let eBay automatically answer common questions for you when buyers inquire about shipping, payment, combined shipping, item details, and returns. eBay answers these questions by responding with the information you provided when listing your items. If you want to add additional info, you can do that as well.

Follow this link to activate your customer faqs.
http://contact.ebay.com/ws/eBayISAPI.dll?ManageSellerFAQ#Shipping

12) Accept returns. Buying online is scary, especially when you are purchasing used items sight unseen. When you offer a money-back guarantee, people feel better about buying from you. Often,

just knowing they can return an item, will give buyers that extra nudge they need to purchase from you.

Many sellers are afraid to offer refunds because they feel it is one more way buyers can take advantage of them. I've offered a 100 percent money back guarantee for the past seven years, and have had fewer than 25 returns in all that time.

If you want to make more sales, offer a "no questions asked" refund policy, and see what it does for your sales.

13) Add video to your listings. It's a fact. People love video. If you can find a way to add videos to your listings, sales are going to go up.

It doesn't have to be a major production. Shoot a quick selfie video from your iPhone talking about your listing. If you've got something cool like a model airplane or remote control car, show someone putting it through its paces.

Keep it simple. Just introduce yourself, and what you like about selling on eBay. It will help build trust in you, which should lead to making more sales.

The best way to add video to your listing is to upload it to YouTube. Use the embed code to paste it into your listing page. Be sure to use the old embed code option. It works best with eBay.

[Come June of 2017, video will no longer be allowed in listings. It is part of eBay's active content ban.]

14) Skip listing upgrades. All they do is put extra money in eBay's pocket. The only one I would suggest is subtitle, and then only when you are selling an expensive item.

What subtitle does is give you an extra eighty characters to help describe your item. Words in your subtitle don't show up in search, but when buyers find your item, it gives extra information that may induce them to click into your listing. Keep in mind, if your item doesn't sell, it's going to cost an extra $1.50 when you relist your item, so be sure to remove the subtitle if you don't want to pay for it again, and again. I don't know how many times I paid the extra fee five or ten times because I forgot all about it.

15) Include tracking information with all your shipments.

Packages get lost. Sometimes buyers say they didn't receive your item when they did. Tracking keeps everybody honest. If buyers don't receive their package, they can open an "item not received case against you."

The first thing eBay does is ask for tracking information. If it shows delivered, you win the case. If you don't have tracking information, eBay will accept the buyer's word that they did not receive your package, and refund the cost of your item plus shipping.

16) Set an insured limit. As a seller, you're responsible until your buyer receives their item. If the buyer doesn't receive the item, or it arrives broken, you are responsible. Set a limit you're comfortable losing. Insure any packages that exceed that amount. One-hundred dollars has always been my limit. If I ship packages valued over one-hundred dollars, I insure them. It limits my losses if something goes wrong.

You also need to keep in mind eBay no longer allows sellers to charge for insurance. You need to roll the cost of insurance into your shipping price, or the price of your item.

17) Sell in a variety of formats. Don't limit yourself to auction, or fixed price listings. Shake things up a bit. Be sure to use best offer and buy-it-now.

If you have a lot of items, try one day, three days, five days, seven day, and ten-day auctions. Offer one item at auction. Sell a few more at fixed price. Tell people in your auction listing if they want the item now, you also have it available with a buy-it-now.

You never know until you try.

Some buyers enjoy the thrill of bidding. They want to score a bargain. Other buyers just want to purchase the item they want and be done with it. Make sure you are catering to both types of buyers.

18) Try new things. Don't be afraid to experiment. Try new products. Keep the ones that sell, discard the ones that don't. Doing

this will keep your inventory fresh, and assure you a constant stream of new products that keep customers coming back to see "what's next."

19) Keep an eye on your competition. If you want to increase your sales, you need to keep an eye on your competition. Watch what they're selling. Keep an eye on any new product offerings they have. Know when they drop a product line. Keep an eye on their prices. Are they going up? Down? Or are they running a string of specials?

Several years ago, my sales dropped significantly for about two months. Finally, it got to the point I needed to figure out what was going on. After a bit of searching, I discovered one of my competitors was getting ready to close his eBay store. He'd dropped his prices from $20.00 each to $2.00, and then $1.00. I couldn't match his prices. But, I did decide this was an opportunity for me to cherry pick his inventory. Over the next few weeks, I grabbed five hundred items that made me a great profit once he was done selling out.

My suggestion is you should make a list of your top five competitors. Keep close tabs on what they're doing. Take notes. Try some of the things they are doing. Over the long run, it will make you a better seller.

20) Set regular office hours. There's a danger to working at home. Because you have everything there, you can be tempted to keep working at it longer than you should. You know what I mean. I just need to list five more sales. I just received a dozen new emails; I better answer them quick.

And, then, there's the biggest time waster of all constantly checking sales. I admit, I still have a problem with this one.

If you can do it, set a time limit. Tell yourself I'm shutting eBay off at 7:00 so I can spend time with my family. So, I can read a good book. So, I can go jogging.

One of the best things you can do is to find a good work/life balance.

21) Read as many books as you can. To be successful, you need to read. Read about how to sell on eBay. Read about what you sell. The more you know about the product line you sell, the more you are going to sell. Buyers love buying from an expert. The more you know about your product line, the more pertinent information you will be able to put in your listings.

If you shop at garage sales, estate sales, or auctions, you're going to recognize bargains, and you should make more money.

22) Write eBay reviews and guides. Share your knowledge with others. eBay guides and reviews give you the opportunity to position yourself as an expert in what you sell.

Writing them doesn't have to be time-consuming.

Do you sell DVD's? Did you watch a new movie? Write a short review telling people what you liked about it. Over time, it's easy to post hundreds of reviews. As reader's stumble across your reviews, many of them will check out your eBay store.

Some may even make a purchase, or two.

Do you sell stamps, coins, or baseball cards?

Millions of collectors visit eBay every day looking for these items. If you write a few guides about grading, collecting tips, how to get the best deal at auction, etc., potential buyers are going to look at you as an expert. Many of them will check out what you're selling.

Use eBay guides and reviews to grow your business.

23) Fill out your eBay profile. Profiles are new to eBay. Like the old MY World, Profiles lets you share information about yourself with other eBay buyers and sellers.

This feature is eBay's attempt to join the social networking revolution. At the top of your Profile page, you can post your profile picture and behind it a banner. You get a short spot to describe your business, and then it shows your feedback.

Below this eBay shows five items you are selling in a scroll bar that allows sellers to look through your items.

The next section is for collections, another new eBay feature. Collections are a Pinterest-like feature that let you build picture collections of items you're selling or other items you like that are selling on eBay.

Below that is a section for followers, and then a larger section that shows your eBay reviews and guides.

My advice is to fill out as much of your eBay Profile as you can. People are more comfortable buying from someone they know—even if they only know you from reading your profile. The more you can show potential buyers you're a real person—the more likely they are to buy from you.

24) End your items often. eBay search favors newly listed items. If you have an eBay store with hundreds or thousands of fixed priced listings, end them often. Instead of using good-till-cancelled, list your items for thirty days. Then relist them—one at a time. It's a pain in the ass, but it will pay off over the long haul.

A ready supply of newly listed items ensures your items stay fresh.

The advantage to you is your items will rise in search each time you relist them. As a result, you will make more sales.

25) Develop an inventory system. One of my biggest challenges occurred about six months after I started selling on eBay. I moved from listing one hundred items to listing over five thousand items.

It became impossible to find items when the time came to ship them. Some days it took me longer to locate the items I sold than it did to print the shipping labels.

When I sold videos, I kept them in boxes scattered all over the basement. Finally, I decided that's enough! I bought a dozen shelves, labeled them from A to Z, and got everything together. It made life a lot easier and saved me over an hour a day in shipping time.

When boxes of videos came in, I scanned them and put them on the proper shelves.

My advice is to develop a good inventory and storage system from day one. It will make your life easier over the long run.

BONUS EXCERPT 5 – USE KICKSTARTER TO FUND AND GROW YOUR BUSINESS

(Here's an excerpt from my book, **Kickstarter for Online Sellers**. This section shows online sellers how to fund special projects using the crowdfunding platform, Kickstarter. You can check the entire book out by following this link, Kickstarter for Online Sellers.)

Most eBay businesses get started with little or no money out of pocket. Sellers begin by listing items they already have around the house. As time goes by, they decide eBay is a pretty decent way to make a few extra bucks.

The next step may be to sell a few things for friends and neighbors. Maybe, they check out a yard sale, garage sale, or local estate sale, and then see what's available at local thrift stores.

If these sellers need financing, it normally comes from their personal credit card.

Up until now, that's been the extent of financing available to eBay sellers. Banks aren't too obliging when they hear the words "eBay" and "business" used together. All too often, negative connotations come to mind, and the banker ends up telling you it's "a great concept, but ____." (You can fill in the blank.)

Kabbage is another financing option available to eBay and Amazon sellers. Kabbage offers small business loans from $500 to $100,000 to online sellers based upon sales data from their eBay and Amazon accounts. Their finance rates aren't cheap. I paid $90.00 in interest and fees on a $500 loan. The good thing is you get the money quickly. Most often, within an hour or less of applying. It's deposited directly into your PayPal account, and payments are deducted from your PayPal account.

If you have a brick and mortar location or a connection with a local banker, more options may open up to you, but for most sellers—the only choice is to use their personal credit card or to get a short-term loan from Kabbage.

....

Crowdfunding is one of the newer financing options available.

At its most basic level, crowdfunding is asking a group of like-minded persons to back you. In essence—you tell them, I have this cool idea for a new way to sell Manga on eBay, but I need a little cash to get it started. In return for their support (money), you reward backers with different incentives. For $5.00, you may give them a shout out on your home page, or a free digital download. For $25.00, you may offer them the first edition of a new Manga. For $250, you could offer them a hand-signed poster from a semi-famous artist, and for $2500, the reward could be an invitation to the online opening of your new store, or maybe you could offer to feature the backer's face somewhere in your store graphics.

The most successful crowdfunding campaign to date was the Veronica Mars Kickstarter in 2013. Producers raised nearly six million dollars from 91,000 backers who couldn't get enough of the TV series. $25 backers received a digital download of the movie. $200 backers received a movie poster hand-signed by the cast and one lucky $10,000 backer received a speaking role in the movie.

In effect, crowdfunding is the coming together of people and an idea. It's a collaboration to make something happen.

For eBay sellers, it's a tougher sell because you're raising money for a commercial product with just one purpose in mind—to make more money. So, if you intend to attract backers, you need to craft one hell of a story.

The Least You Need to Know

The least you need to know about Kickstarter https://www.kickstarter.com/ is you're either "all in, " or you're "all out."

If you set your goal at $10,000, you don't get one cent if you don't raise at least $10,000. If you raise $9999, you're out of luck. None of those credit cards get charged, and you walk away empty handed.

Think it can't happen to you?

More than 55 percent of the projects listed on Kickstarter don't reach their goal. The numbers are even gloomier when you look at all crowdfunding platforms—25 percent of all projects listed don't receive even one cent in backing.

How scary is that?

I'm not telling you this to discourage you from running a Kickstarter; rather I'm trying to help you understand how important it is to have a plan and thoroughly research your project before you get started.

The first thing you need to know about Kickstarter is it's not about getting money to fund your business. It's about getting money to fund a project.

So, if you need to raise $100,000 so you can start selling iPhones on eBay, it's not going to happen. Not on Kickstarter anyway. If your business makes custom cases for the iPhone 5 and 6, with custom graphics, or a hot new design you created, Kickstarter just might be the ticket to help you launch your business.

The reason custom iPhone cases could get funded is it's a unique project. If your graphics are cool enough, or if the design is unique and stands out head and shoulders over what's available on the market—it just may go viral and grab the interest of backers.

Here's another example.

If you ask for $25,000 to start an online CD store, you're unlikely to attract any backers, except your mom and your Uncle Bob (and even they may be a hard sell). If you're the lead singer in a local or regional band, and you could run a Kickstarter to raise the cash to press your first CD. That could grab a whole lot of backers, as would a CD of local school kids singing regional folk songs or Christmas carols.

Do you see the difference?

A Kickstarter is something you use to launch a special one-time project, not to fund an ongoing business. That's not to say you can't fund a string of similar projects that turn into an entire product line for your eBay store. If you run a successful Kickstarter to fund a CD for a local band, there's nothing to stop you from running another Kickstarter for the same band's next album, or an entire run of albums for many local or regional bands.

It's all about breaking your goal down into a series of attainable projects.

Getting funded

What if you ran a Kickstarter and nobody came? It'd be embarrassing, wouldn't it?

Remember those statistics I gave you earlier—25 percent of all crowdfunding projects never receive one penny in backing, and 55 percent of Kickstarter's never launch.

Here's a tip I heard over, and over again, from successful, and unsuccessful Kickstarters. Ask for the smallest amount of money necessary to get your project off the ground. We all want a million dollars, but if ten thousand dollars will help your project achieve liftoff, set your goal at ten thousand dollars. You may get a whole lot more; you may not. But if you hit $10,000 Kickstarter is going to run all those credit cards, and ka-ching! You're in the money!

That's the great thing about Kickstarter. They don't shut the faucet off when you reach your goal. Some projects go on to raise five or ten times their initial goal. And, that's another thing successful Kickstarter's say, try to have enough momentum going into your project so that you can meet your goal in the first three days. That way anything else you take in is just frosting on the cake.

What You Need to Know

- Kickstarter reviews and vets all projects. Your odds of being approved are roughly 50 percent. If you've got a sustainable idea, but they think it needs a little work, the folks at Kickstarter will give you tips to make it more fundable.
- Choose a time frame for your Kickstarter. It can be as short as one day, but no more than sixty days. Keep in mind—longer is not always better. Kickstarter says projects attract the most backers during their first three days, and last three days, so it's those six days that make or break your project. Sellers say thirty days are the sweet spot, any longer and you encourage backers to procrastinate, and possibly miss funding your project.
- Remember, you're asking people to help you, but it's not going to work if you come right out and beg for help. Instead, you need to show backers how your project can help other people, or help them. Make sure backers understand; it's not about the cash; it's about being part of something new and exciting—like bringing back Veronica Mars.
- Video is the key. A fancy video is nice, but it's more important to get out there in front of the camera and be yourself. Be genuine, explain your project in terms people can relate to.
- One video isn't going to be enough. You need a series of videos. Create one or two videos that explain your project. Try to get a couple of your backers to talk about your project, and what excited, or intrigued them about it. As your project progresses, create several videos to update people on your status. "We're almost there." "We're so close, and every donation you make will bring us that much closer to hitting our goal." Or, "we just created a new stretch goal so be sure

to check out our new reward levels." Or, "here's what hitting our new goal will let us achieve."

- Tell backers why it's important for them to help you. Let them know why you need their help, what's in it for them, and what will happen when you hit your goal. Remember, if backers don't understand why they need to contribute, your project isn't going to get off the ground.
- Creative rewards are important to getting more backers, and funding your project. You need several different levels of rewards to achieve liftoff. At the low end, you can give a shout out on your blog or website, or offer a digital download. The midrange--$25 to $50—is the perfect spot to offer a custom t-shirt, an autographed book or something with a higher perceived value. At the high end, over $100—you need unique rewards that make backers feel they're a part of something special, and that their contribution is going to help make it happen. The best way I heard it described was to decide what it's going to take to get someone to give up a latte, or dinner and a movie out, and help them justify why they should forgo some of life's little pleasures to back you instead.
- Professional quality pictures are essential. You've got to show your project in its best light—up-close, with people using it if possible. Make sure your pictures and videos tell the story. Most backers are just going to look at your pictures, and contribute based on what they see. Others will decide from looking at pictures and videos, whether they're going to read your text to get the rest of the story.
- If things go totally wrong, and you don't hit your goal, it's not the end of the world. Be a gracious loser. Email your backers, and thank them for their support. If you lined up a different source of funding in the meantime, let backers know your project is going to move forward despite the

setback on Kickstarter. Whatever you do, let your backers know what's next—a new Kickstarter, or maybe a scaled back version of your project.
- Whether your project gets funded or not, take time out to analyze your Kickstarter. What went well? Where did it all fall apart? It's not a total loss if you can learn from your mistakes. If no one backed your project, you might need to approach it from a new angle, or you may decide it's time to move on, and try something different. It may be that even though you didn't hit your goal, you created enough publicity that you can pick up commercial financing or a new set of backers. Whatever you do, don't just throw in the towel without taking the time to analyze what happened.

Kickstarter – The Nuts & Bolts

Setting up a Kickstarter is pretty straightforward. Navigate your way to https://www.kickstarter.com/. Click on *learn more*, and then *start a project*. Kickstarter will show you the following sentence. "I want to start a_____ project called _____." Fill in the two blanks, and you're ready to get started.

There are fifteen categories to choose from for your project type: arts, comics, crafts, dance, design, fashion, film and video, food, games, journalism, music, photography, publishing, technology, and theater.

The most successful categories are film and video, music, design, games, art, and publishing. If you choose a project that fits into one of these categories, you are more likely to get funded.

Next, you need to give your project a title. Don't try to be cutesy or clever, instead, explain your project so people can easily understand it. If you're a local band, title it "Davenport, Iowa River Rats premiere CD," or "Pictorial History of Black Hawk State Park."

After you enter the title, you're taken to the product page. This is where the magic starts to come together. Before you begin, make sure you understand what each step is asking you to do.

First off, you need to upload a project image. It's the money shot. It's how people will judge your project. It needs to grab the attention of potential backers, and entice them to keep scrolling down the page. Kickstarter recommends your picture should be at least 1024x768 pixels and have a 4:3 aspect ratio.

Next, you get a shot at revising your title. You've only got sixty characters to work with—so make them count. Don't mince words, or try and be clever. Your title needs to be clear, concise, and contain two or three keywords that tell people what your project is all about. Hint: Your title is searchable by keyword along with your name, so this is one of the ways people are going to find you. Make it easy for backers to find your Kickstarter, and you will attract more donations.

The next space asks for a short blurb—just 135 characters. It needs to whet someone's appetite, and make them want to keep scrolling down the page to discover what's next?

After this, you pick a category and sub-category for your project. Then, you set your location. I think location is one of the key areas, especially if you have a regional following. It's one of Kickstarter's real strengths. Backers can search through projects to locate Kickstarter's in their hometown, state, or region, so you want to make sure they can key in on you.

After location, you need to pick a funding duration. That's just a fancy way of asking how long you want your Kickstarter to run. Thirty days is the suggested sweet spot, but you can make it as short as one day, or as-long-as 60 days. Most backers pick up on a project in its first three days and its final three days. These are the days you need to be pushing the hardest.

The final thing you need to do is set your funding goal. Remember, you may want $100,000, but if $10,000 will launch your project, that's the amount you should set for your goal. Kickstarter is an "all, or nothing," platform. If you don't reach your funding goal, you don't get anything—no matter how much was pledged.

That's as far as I'm going to take you with setting up your Kickstarter. They have an awesome section to walk you through telling your story. You can access it by following this link. https://www.kickstarter.com/help/handbook/your_story.

Getting the Word Out

So, you've created a Kickstarter—now what?

Just about every person I talked with who created a Kickstarter offered the same advice. Running your campaign is a full-time job. It requires planning, research, and constant getting out there 24 / 7 to share your story.

The sad truth is, Kickstarter is only going to bring you ten to fifteen percent of your backers. It's up to you find the other 85 percent of your funding. Sounds sort of like what I told you about eBay, doesn't it? **Kickstarter is a platform where you can share your crowdfunding project. Getting the word out is up to you**.

Here the top ten tips I discovered to help you run a more successful Kickstarter.

- Build your tribe before you get started. To be successful you need an email list, and a substantial Twitter and Facebook following. That way when you start your Kickstarter, you can have them jump in and be your initial wave of backers.
- You need to research other Kickstarter's in your category to see how they're approaching things. Learn from what they're doing right; eliminate the mistakes they're making.
- Go local. If you're a local band, musician, writer, manufacturer whatever, reach out to the local media. Get as much publicity as you can. Submit press releases. Get on local TV and radio programs, and seek out opportunities for write-ups in the newspapers and local magazines.

- Reach out to niche bloggers. Offer to do interviews, guests posts, or provide free content for them. If possible, work out a trade where you can do something for them, if they email their list with details about your Kickstarter.
- Ask family, friends, and work associates to help get the word out on their social networks. You never know, they may have the ear of an influencer who can help your Kickstarter go viral.
- Rewards are important to your success. Kickstarter says $25.00 is the most common backing, and $70.00 is the average backing. What that tells you is you need to focus a lot of sweet rewards in the $25.00 to $75.00 range. You don't have to break the bank, but give them a high perceived value—a special edition of a CD, book, or print, a hand signed t-shirt, or whatever you feel your audience will value more than the backing you are requesting.
- Keep adding content to your Kickstarter page. Research shows many backers sneak two or three peeks at your story before they decide to back you. Be sure to add new content, especially more videos and pictures. Update your page to let backers know how close you are to reaching your goal, or about new stretch goals and rewards, if you've already reached your initial goal. The main thing is to keep backers in the loop.
- Back a few projects before you post yours. It provides social proof that you play well with others. Kickstarter has a spot at the top of each project page that shows how many projects you've backed. If that spot is blank, it makes you appear somewhat like Mr. Scrooge. You're looking for handouts, but you're not willing to help out. "Bah! Hum-bug, Mr. Scrooge!"
- You need to show why you're the best person to complete the project you posted. Tell backers what's special about

you. What makes you the right guy to get this thing done? Have you tackled a similar project? Share your motivation, so people understand you're the right guy, or gal, for the job.
- You can lose, and still, come out a winner. Just because you didn't get the funding, you asked for doesn't make you a loser (it just means you'll have to try a little harder). A successful Kickstarter can generate a lot of publicity that will help grow your business down the line. It can be a great conversation starter. "We didn't get funded, but we got a lot of great responses." Or, "we learned…" It might provide the feedback you need to come back with an improved and even better product.

IF YOU ENJOYED THIS BOOK

Thank you for reading this book. If you enjoyed it or found it helpful, I'd be grateful if you'd post a short review where you purchased it. Your review does help. It helps other readers decide if this book would be a good investment for them, and it helps me to make this an even better book for you. I read all the reviews my books receive and based on what readers tell me; I can make my books even better, and include the kind of information readers want and need.

Here's a link to this book on Amazon Kindle.

https://www.amazon.com/dp/B01NCIIO8G/ref=sr_1_2?s=books&ie=UTF8&qid=1480965527&sr=1-2&keywords=ecommerce+2017

Thanks again for choosing my book, and here's wishing you great sales on eBay.

....

Want to know about Nick's new book releases? Join our mailing list.

Interested in being notified when Nick releases his next book? Click here to join our mailing list. We promise not to send any spam or unwanted emails. The only thing you will receive is news about Nick's new book releases and occasional specials we are offering.

www.ingramcontent.com/pod-product-compliance
Lightning Source LLC
Chambersburg PA
CBHW020915180526
45163CB00007B/2750